Navigating Foreignerness

Stories of Cultural Adaptation and Belonging

Copyright

ISBN: 9798345604830

Published by The Culture Factor Group Oy

Copyright © 2024 by Egbert Schram.
All rights reserved.

2nd edition. August 2025

No part of this book may be reproduced, distributed, or transmitted in any form or by any means, including photocopying, recording, or other electronic or mechanical methods, without the prior written permission of the publisher, except in the case of brief quotations embodied in critical reviews and certain other noncommercial uses permitted by copyright law.

For permission requests, contact the publisher at:
sales@theculturefactor.com

Editorial work: Deron Fuller (Fuller Interactions)
Visual design: Emmi Kytsonen (Karppi Design)

Thank you to: Marita S, Gijs B, Nathan G, Marcel K, Rianne S, John P, Joe Mc S, Chris vd W, Julia W, Elina W, Watze de W, Igor M, Sead B, Petri R, Marco M for test reading and the interviews.

Disclaimer

The information in this book is intended for general informational purposes only. While every effort has been made to ensure that the information provided is accurate and up-to-date, the author and publisher make no warranties or representations of any kind regarding the completeness, accuracy, or reliability of the content. This book should not be used as a substitute for professional advice or guidance in specific situations.

The views and opinions expressed in this book are those of the author and do not necessarily reflect the views of any organization or individuals mentioned. Any reliance you place on the information is strictly at your own risk. The author and publisher disclaim any liability for any loss, damage, or harm arising from the use or misuse of the information contained in this book.

The scenarios described in this book are based on field interviews conducted with the interviewed persons and subsequently interpreted through the expert eye of the author of this book.

About the author

Egbert Schram is the Group CEO of The Culture Factor Group and a transformative leader with a track record of turning challenges into success stories. Over 12 years, he has grown The Culture Factor Group with 240%, and similarly helped customers increase Year to Year turnover with up to 29%, reduce customer support workload with 33%, reduce customer's involuntary attrition rates with 16%. As such he demonstrates a unique ability to align organizational culture with strategic goals.

A trusted advisor to organizations ranging from the UNDP, Al Ghurair Group, Unilever, Coca Cola, Airbus, Schulte Group, Huhtamäki, Onlogic and a range of other organizations, Egbert is passionate about building emotionally sustainable workplaces that empower people and fuel long-term success.

With an active presence on LinkedIn and a knack for storytelling, he brings insights on culture, strategy, and human connection to life.

Foreword

In our increasingly interconnected world, understanding national cultures has never been more essential. Cultural identities, deeply rooted in history and tradition, shape how individuals see the world, communicate, and build relationships. As we work, travel, and collaborate across borders, recognizing both the similarities and differences among cultures enhances our interactions, fostering mutual respect and understanding in a meaningful way.

This book offers a unique exploration of the dimensions of culture and examines how our individual cultural tendencies either harmonize with or diverge from those around us. It's a quantitative, fact-based guide that maps our cultural orientations and highlights how they align or clash with the environments we inhabit.

As someone who has long appreciated the subtleties of cultural diversity, I know that understanding these dynamics fosters not only knowledge but also a deeper empathy for others. Having lived and worked across multiple countries over the past three decades, I have seen firsthand how this knowledge can help us manage ourselves and our relationships more effectively.

Egbert Schram, with his extensive expertise in cultural studies and practice, is uniquely positioned to lead us on this journey. Through meticulous research and a commitment to accuracy, he has created a resource that is both informative and engaging.

I encourage readers to approach this book with an open heart and mind. Embracing cultures beyond our own can challenge our assumptions and expand our worldview. As you explore the pages ahead, may you gain not only knowledge but also inspiration from the intricate beauty of cultural heritage worldwide.

Pinaki Dutt
- Former global head of connected intelligence Mediacom
- Former global head of marketing effectiveness Coca Cola
- Global CMK head Ornua Dairy

Contents

Contents

About the author 3

Foreword 5

Contents 7

Part 1: Theoretical background 11

Introduction: We are all foreigners in one way or another. 12

   The Culture Factor: Understanding Foreignerness through Culture 14

   Exploring Foreignerness through Personal Stories 15

   The Goal of This Book 16

Introducing the 6 Dimensions of National Culture 18

   What is National Culture? 18

   The 6 Dimensions of National Culture in a nutshell 22

   Why These Dimensions Matter 28

   Applying the 6 Dimensions 29

   Keep in mind 29

Part 2: Stories 31

Story 1 - Initial exposure to foreignerness 32

   Understanding of a journey 36

   Overall Reflection 40

Story 2: Navigating Identity and Work in a Global Context

....42

    Understanding of a journey..47

    Overall Reflection 51

Story 3 - Team Building Challenges at Teravamuoti.........53

    Understanding of a journey..58

    Overall Reflection 62

Story 4 From Florida to Finland – The Eastern route........64

    Understanding of a journey..69

    Overall Reflection 73

Story 5 – Navigating Leadership and Communication in a Global Context...74

    Understanding of a journey..79

    Overall Reflection 84

Story 6 Navigating Identity and Career in Post-War Bosnia-Herzegovina..85

    Understanding of a journey..91

    Overall Reflection 95

Story 7 Embracing Multiculturalism and Flexibility in Leadership 97

    Understanding of a journey..102

    Overall Reflection 107

Story 8 Via Veneto - Navigating Italy and Japan.............108

    Understanding of a journey..115

    Overall Reflection 119

Story 9 Navigating Identity and Leadership – A Journey

from Cork to Corporate America 121

    Understanding of a journey 127

    Overall Reflection 131

Story 10: Embracing Change – A Journey from Finland to the World 132

    Understanding of a journey 137

    Overall Reflection 142

Part 3: Strategies 143

Ten Key Takeaways on Adapting When You Feel Out of Place 144

Recommendations for Organisations: Learning from the 10 Lessons on Adapting to Cultural Differences 149

Conclusion: Moving Towards a Culturally Inclusive Future 153

Final thoughts 163

Part 1: Theoretical background

Introduction: We are all foreigners in one way or another.

"Buitenlander," "Auslander," "Ulkomaalainen"— three words from different languages, all describing the concept of a "foreigner" as someone who comes from another country. Yet, the experience of being a foreigner goes beyond just crossing national borders; it extends into the realms of culture, identity, and belonging. This book explores how cultural differences shape our understanding of what it means to be a foreigner, not just in terms of nationality, but in the broader sense of feeling out of place, whether at home or abroad.

Having lived abroad myself for nearly two decades by the time this book is published, I have often pondered what makes one feel "at home" when others see you as different. Is it easier to create a sense of belonging in societies where the word for "foreigner" is less focused on nationality and more on the integration of the individual?

The English word "foreigner" and the French "étranger" seem to carry less judgment, suggesting that as long as one integrates, they can become part of the British, Canadian, American, or French fabric.

We may find ourselves navigating new cultures, unfamiliar environments, or even unexpected differences within our own communities.

This book aims to shed light on the complexities of these experiences by exploring the lives of 10 individuals who have lived in over 20 countries.

Through their stories, we delve into the concept of "foreignerness" and how it intersects with culture, identity, and belonging.

I have coined the concept of "foreignerness" to stretch beyond the traditional meaning of "beyond national borders.

The narratives in this book are not just about the challenges of being a foreigner in a new country; they are also about the deeper, more subtle forms of foreignerness we experience in our everyday lives.

Whether it's adjusting to a new corporate culture, adapting to societal norms in a different region, or simply feeling out of sync with the prevailing values of a place, the sense of being an outsider is something we all grapple with at some point.

The Culture Factor: Understanding Foreignerness through Culture

At the heart of this exploration is the concept of The Culture Factor—a framework for understanding how basic human needs, group influence, and personality intersect within specific cultural contexts. This book does not seek to offer one-size-fits-all solutions. Instead, it encourages readers to ask questions which prompt deeper thinking about the unique cultural dynamics at play in their own lives and organizations.

Culture is often talked about in terms of national or organizational culture, but these distinctions are not always clear-cut. National culture plays a crucial role in shaping organizational culture, and vice versa. Understanding this interplay is essential for anyone navigating cross-cultural environments, whether in personal or professional settings.

The Culture Factor emphasizes that cultural understanding should work for you, not against you. It should be a competitive advantage that helps you achieve your goals, rather than a barrier that hinders progress. This book explores how to leverage cultural differences effectively, whether by creating more inclusive workplaces, fostering a sense of belonging, or navigating the complexities of cultural identity.

Exploring Foreignerness through Personal Stories

Each chapter in this book presents the story of a protagonist who has experienced foreignerness in different ways. These stories are followed by a reflection on the cultural dynamics at play, using a behavioural model to analyze the situations.

The aim is to offer insights that can help readers make better strategic choices when it comes to cultural issues.

For example, the story of Kalle, a leader navigating cultural differences within a rapidly growing organization, highlights the challenges of aligning personal values with corporate culture. Dino's journey from war-torn Bosnia to a global career showcases the impact of cultural identity on professional development. Anni's experiences in China and her subsequent career in Europe demonstrate the complexities of cultural adaptation and the importance of inclusivity.

By examining these stories through the lens of The Culture Factor, this book aims to uncover the underlying cultural dynamics that influence our sense of foreignness and belonging.

The final chapter will synthesize the key takeaways, providing practical insights for those moving across borders or collaborating with people from different cultural backgrounds.

The Goal of This Book

The goal of this book is to leave you with more questions than answers. In a world that is too complex for best practices to be universally applicable, the only true best practice is to ask the right questions. By engaging with the stories and reflections in this book, you will be better equipped to navigate the cultural challenges in your own life and work.

Ultimately, this book is about creating societies and organizations where those who are different, in whichever sense of the word, have the opportunity to participate fully and are not judged based on their differences. It is about recognizing that we are all foreigners in some way and that by embracing our differences, we can build stronger, more inclusive communities.

As you read through the following chapters, I encourage you to reflect on your own experiences of foreignerness and consider how cultural dynamics have shaped your identity and interactions with others. By doing so, you can gain a deeper understanding of The Culture Factor and its impact on the concept of foreignerness in our increasingly interconnected world.

This understanding comes by mapping your own cultural value preferences, something you can do by purchasing The Culture Compass assessment from The Culture Factor Group: https://www.theculturefactor.com/solutions/the-culture-compass

Introducing the 6 Dimensions of National Culture

Understanding culture is essential for navigating the complexities of today's globalized world, whether in personal interactions, business environments, or societal structures. Culture is not just about food, language, or traditions; it is deeply embedded in the way people think, behave, and interact with one another.

To explore this further, this chapter introduces the 6 dimensions of national culture, a framework developed by Dutch social psychologist Geert Hofstede, and further developed at the organization I lead, The Culture Factor Group.

These dimensions provide a powerful tool for understanding how cultural values shape behaviors, expectations, and interactions in different countries.

What is National Culture?

National culture refers to the collective programming of the mind that distinguishes the members of one nation from those of another. It encompasses the values, beliefs, and norms shared by people within a specific country. National culture influences how individuals perceive the world, how they interact with others, and how they make decisions. It is deeply rooted in the history, geography, and social structure of a country, and it evolves over time.

Hofstede's research into national culture began in the 1970s, and his findings have been instrumental in helping individuals and organizations understand the impact of cultural differences on behaviour.

The 6 Dimensions of National Culture he identified provide a framework for comparing the cultural values of different countries. Initially built around four distinct clusters of answers to specific questions, two more dimensions were added between 2005 and 2009. Further research was done between 2016 and 2023 by The Culture Factor Group.

In this book, we refer to pre-2023 scores as the people I interviewed were mostly born before 1985. Scores representing the national culture at that time can be found here:
https://www.theculturefactor.com/country-comparison-legacy

In chapter seven, we've built a description of what would happen if and when you'd be managing a diverse team such as the combined ten people I interviewed.

An important note to make here - National culture

scores are to personal value preferences as the wealth of a country compared to individual wealth. They are connected, but not the same.

So why do we use personal scores in this book and compare them to countries?

> *The reason is to help you as a reader reflect deeper on how culture might influence you.*

You are not your country's statistical average, as each interviewee shows. At the same time, most interviewees do closely resemble the average score of their country.

In the end, when you work with people who have a different background to you (as most will, in one way or the other), understanding the individual's value preferences helps you to anticipate how, where and when culture might influence you.

So, keep your eyes, ears and heart open and embrace the differences, learn how to wield the differences to make a positive impact!

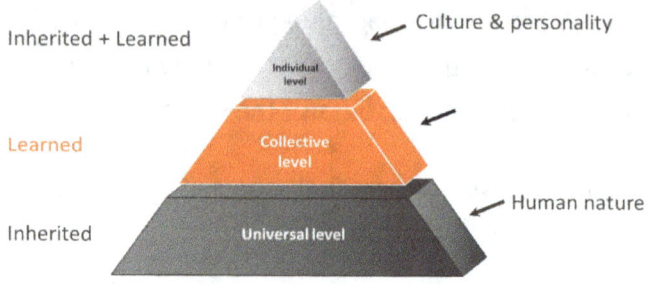

Graph: The Culture Factor exists across layers of human nature

Culture is the phenomenon occurring between the individual and humanity - it is our socially embedded way of looking at the world around us.

At The Culture Factor we try to assist our customers by building bridges between these three different layers, keeping in mind that as people we all need to:

1. Feel appreciated
2. Feel a sense of belonging and
3. Need a sense of purpose

We just express these needs in different ways depending on where we were born and raised, and to a certain extent our personality.

This book is not about humanity, nor is it about individual personality; instead, it is about the interaction between the interviewee's stories and the cultures they encountered.

The 6 Dimensions of National Culture in a nutshell

You can read more about the 6 Dimensions on the website www.theculturefactor.com. In a nutshell, from a work context, you might recognize these dimensions by looking at the examples below.

1. *Power Distance (PDI)*

Metaphor: Power Distance acts as the brake or accelerator of hierarchy.

In cultures with high Power Distance (e.g., Malaysia), hierarchy is like a red light that you don't question—you slow down when approaching authority. It signals that decisions flow from the top, and deviating from that chain is both uncomfortable and inappropriate.

In contrast, low Power Distance cultures (e.g., Denmark) treat hierarchy more like a speed bump than a traffic light—present, but not limiting. People can accelerate past layers of authority if it helps them move faster or get things done more efficiently.

At work: A high-PDI employee may hesitate to speak up or challenge a superior, while a low-PDI employee may comfortably bypass formalities if they believe it will lead to better results.

2. Individualism vs Collectivism (IDV)

Metaphor: Individualism is a gas pedal on personal initiative; Collectivism is a brake on self-expression in favor of group cohesion.

In individualist cultures (e.g., the Netherlands), the message is "go ahead"—the road is open for you to express yourself, stand out, and assert your views. Individual responsibility fuels speed and innovation.

In collectivist cultures (e.g., Vietnam), social norms act like a speed governor—limiting how fast or how far one can go alone. Harmony, group consensus, and respect for relationships create a controlled environment where acceleration is only encouraged if the group approves.

At work: A Dutch employee might openly critique a team decision; a Vietnamese employee might hold back until they've checked how the group feels.

3. Motivation towards Achievement and Success (MAS)

Metaphor: This dimension modulates how hard we press the gas pedal in pursuit of success—or whether we even feel the need to race.

In high MAS cultures (e.g., Japan), the accelerator is pressed firmly—people strive for excellence, set high benchmarks, and may define their identity by their achievements.

In low MAS cultures (e.g., Sweden), the foot eases off the pedal. Life is not a race, and cooperation, equality, and well-being often take precedence over winning or outperforming others.

At work: In high-MAS environments, employees may compete intensely for recognition; in low-MAS settings, they may collaborate more and avoid standing out.

4. Uncertainty Avoidance Index (UAI)

Metaphor: High UAI is a brake on spontaneity, while low UAI releases the clutch and allows for freewheeling.

In cultures with high Uncertainty Avoidance (e.g., Greece), people tend to drive cautiously—avoiding detours and unknown paths. Structure, rules, and predictability are essential for comfort and control.

In low UAI cultures (e.g., Singapore), there's more of a green-light mentality: take the scenic route, adapt as you go, and learn from the ride. These cultures are more accepting of experimentation and ambiguity.

At work: A Greek team might demand detailed plans before starting a project; a Singaporean team might start and adjust on the fly.

5. Long-Term Orientation vs. Short-Term Normative Orientation (LTO)

Metaphor: LTO decides whether you're driving with the long view in mind or reacting to what's just ahead.

Long-Term Oriented cultures (e.g., China) drive like GPS users—always optimizing for future distance and sustainability. Delayed gratification, patience, and adaptability are the norms.

Short-Term Oriented cultures (e.g., the USA) tend to follow road signs they already know—anchored in traditions, pride, and short-term results. The focus is on today's win, not next decade's return.

At work: Chinese firms may invest heavily in R&D with no immediate payoff; American firms might prioritize quarterly performance or rapid scaling.

6. Indulgence vs. Restraint (IVR)

Metaphor: Indulgence is like driving with the windows down and music up; Restraint drives in quiet, focused moderation.

In indulgent cultures (e.g., Mexico), the emotional gas pedal is often pressed—they celebrate, express joy, and follow impulses more freely. Life is to be enjoyed.

In restrained cultures (e.g., Ukraine), emotional restraint acts as a governor—pleasure is not openly prioritized, and gratification is more carefully regulated or even viewed with suspicion.

At work: In indulgent settings, workplace celebrations and optimistic messaging may be common; in restrained environments, discipline and modesty dominate both communication and reward systems.

Why These Dimensions Matter

Thinking of the 6 dimensions as behavioral traffic controls helps leaders and teams better navigate the dynamics of working across borders.

It also highlights that no dimension is "better" or "worse", it is just a different rhythm of when to accelerate, brake, or cruise depending on the cultural road you're driving on.

These dimensions help explain why people from different cultures may have different approaches to work, communication, and relationships. For example, understanding that a colleague from a high-Power Distance culture may be less likely to challenge authority can help in managing expectations and fostering better teamwork.

These dimensions also provide insights into how national culture influences organizational culture. Organizations that operate in multiple countries must navigate these cultural differences to create cohesive and effective teams. For example, a global company might need to adapt a regional management style to accommodate both high and low Power Distance cultures within its workforce.

Applying the 6 Dimensions

Throughout this book, we will explore the real-life implications of these cultural dimensions through the stories of individuals who have navigated cross-cultural environments.

- By examining how these dimensions play out in different contexts, we aim to provide practical insights that can help you understand and bridge cultural gaps in your own life and work.
- By applying this framework, you can develop a deeper appreciation for the diversity of human experience and learn how to navigate the challenges and opportunities that arise in a multicultural world.

The importance for organizations lies in understanding that working in ways which go counter to these emotional preferences is a recipe for disaster - financial and social. Therefore, in the final chapter I sum up the book with a couple of key takeaways from both an individual and organizational point of view.

Keep in mind

Overall, it is assumed that people's cultural value preferences remain quite stable, assuming their environment stays quite stable. Moving to a new country can be a challenging and life-changing event, so it is not unlikely that our interviewees' value preferences have changed throughout their life.

We describe "Culture fit" as the culture where you fit most, as there will never be a perfect fit. The way to calculate the Culture fit is by calculating the aggregated gap between your personal score (by taking the Culture Compass assessment) and your comparison countries.

If a gap on any dimension is more than 15 points, you can expect that you will feel this in your gut; if there are big gaps on all dimensions, the likelihood is large that you will struggle to adapt, and the threshold for leaving will be quite low.

So, to summarize the introduction, take this book and the way we apply the scores as mental exercise in terms of what people might expect when encountering other cultures, nothing more, nothing less.

Part 2: Stories

Story 1 - Initial exposure to foreignerness

Jan was born in the early '60s as the second child of a Dutch father and mother who belonged to a Calvinist church. His older sister was born in Bogotá, Colombia. His younger brother and sister were both born, like Jan, in the Netherlands. Nowadays, Jan lives and blooms in Finland.

Early Childhood

Jan's conception was in the vibrant and bustling city of Bogotá, Colombia, where his mother exposed him for six months to Latin-American music and dance while still in the womb. The family moved back to the

Netherlands, and he continued to have a life filled with rich culture and diverse experiences. Their father's work took the family to various places, exposing Jan to different cultures and environments that in the last century still existed throughout the Netherlands. This nomadic lifestyle shaped his worldview from a young age, teaching him adaptability and resilience.

The Move to the Netherlands

The family initially moved to Utrecht, where Jan was born, and subsequently to four different villages in the west and north part of the country by the time he had reached the age of 10. The family's next significant move was to the south of the Netherlands, a transition that marked a profound shift in Jan's life. Settling in the town of Bergeijk, which had a strong Catholic presence, presented unique challenges for Jan, who was Protestant. One particular story from this time stands out: the local tradition of playing football on Sundays. As a Protestant, Jan was excluded from this social activity, highlighting the subtle but impactful ways religious differences can affect social integration.

Despite this early exclusion, Jan's educational journey in the Netherlands was a different story. During his studies, he mingled with a diverse group of people, and in this environment, his background did not matter. It was a time of exploration and acceptance, where he learned the value of diversity and inclusiveness. It was also during these years that he met his first wife, a Dutch Catholic.

Post-Doctoral Life in the USA

After completing their studies, Jan and his wife moved to the USA for their post-doctoral work. The American experience was a more uncomfortable one. The social context in the USA was heavily influenced by religion, and this made building a social network challenging for them. They felt like outsiders in a society where social connections were often formed within religious communities. Moreover, the stark wealth inequalities in the USA were a shock to Jan, highlighting the deep societal divides that existed.

Challenges of Integration in Belgium

Following their stint in the USA, Jan and his wife moved to Belgium. Here, too, integration proved to be difficult. Despite these challenges, their children were born and raised in Belgium, and Jan noticed how their upbringing in this environment influenced their behaviour. His children became less confrontational and more accepting of hierarchy, reflecting the cultural norms of Belgian society.

The hierarchical nature of Belgian society also impacted Jan and his wife professionally. His wife, an immunologist, faced significant challenges working under a Belgian haematologist who would often demean her by calling her an "unbelievable Dutch person." In contrast, her Chinese subordinates navigated this hierarchy more smoothly by outwardly agreeing ("yes") while quietly doing things their own way. This difference in approach highlighted the complexities of working within different cultural frameworks.

Finding Comfort in Finland

Jan's move to Finland brought a refreshing change, as Jan mentioned:

"Finnish culture, with its characteristic directness and respect for personal space, felt much easier to understand."

The Finnish way of giving people the space to observe and acclimate was a welcome contrast to the more hierarchical and rigid environments Jan had experienced before.

Professional Fulfilment

Throughout his career, Jan found his greatest professional fulfilment in mentoring programs. These programs allowed him to help others feel at ease, fostering an environment of support and growth. Mentoring became a cornerstone of his work, reflecting his commitment to inclusivity and the value of diverse perspectives.

Understanding of a journey

Jan's Culture Compass scores compared to the values of the Dutch and Finnish culture (both older and newer data) and some of the countries he has worked with, gives us the table below. For the explanation of the abbreviations please refer to the introduction page of this book. Jan's scores:

Scores of selected countries based around the time of his movements.

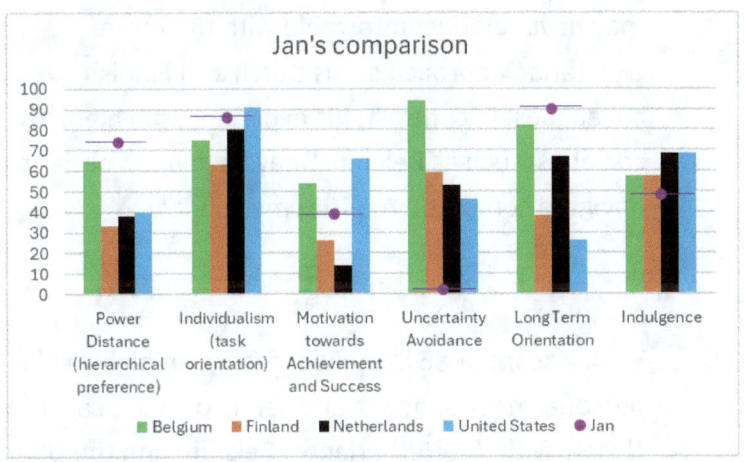

Reflection on Jan's Culture Scores

Jan's journey from the Netherlands to various

countries, including the USA, Belgium, and Finland, highlights his adaptability and resilience in navigating diverse cultural landscapes. By examining Jan's Culture Compass scores and comparing them to the values of Dutch and Finnish cultures, as well as other countries he has worked with, we gain deeper insights into how cultural dynamics have influenced his experiences and personal growth.

Power Distance Index (PDI)

Jan's score of 74 in Power Distance indicates a relatively high tolerance for hierarchical structures and an acceptance of unequal power distribution. This score is significantly higher than the Dutch score (38) and even further from the Finnish score (33). Jan may have felt uncomfortable with the more egalitarian approach of his Dutch and Finnish colleagues. In contrast, his experiences in hierarchical societies, such as Belgium, may have been easier to navigate compared to his home country.

Individualism vs. Collectivism (IDV)

With a score of 86 in Individualism, Jan highly values personal independence and self-expression, aligning closely with the Netherlands, Belgium and the USA, while Finland shows a moderate alignment. This strong alignment indicates that Jan is comfortable in cultures that prioritise individual rights and personal freedom. The close match with these cultural norms likely made his adaptation to these environments smoother.

Assertiveness (MAS)

Jan's score of 39 in assertiveness reflects a moderate preference for cooperation, modesty, and quality of life over competitiveness and assertiveness. This score is higher than both the Dutch (14) and Finnish (26) scores, which indicates that while Jan values balance between competition and care, he is more competitive than average in these cultures, yet much less competitive when compared with the USA (62) and Belgium (54).

His preference for environments where teamwork, collaboration, and inclusivity are prioritised such as his fulfilment in mentoring programs, may have met challenges from both sides of the spectrum.

Given that he is in the middle of all three target countries with his personal preference, Jan had to find a coping mechanism to balance the differences.

Uncertainty Avoidance Index (UAI)

Jan's score of 2 in Uncertainty Avoidance is extremely low, indicating a high tolerance for ambiguity and a preference for flexibility and spontaneity. This score is much lower than the scores of his comparison countries. His low score likely helped him navigate the complexities of living in various countries and adapting to different cultural environments. However, the significant gaps with the other countries suggest that Jan may have occasionally struggled with the more structured and risk-averse aspects of these societies, potentially feeling constrained by their preference for predictability and order, while his colleagues might have found Jan's approach too chaotic, in other words lacking predictability which could have led to them feeling anxious.

Long-Term Orientation vs. Short-Term Normative Orientation (LTO)

Jan's score of 90 in Long-Term Orientation reflects a strong focus on future planning, perseverance, and long-term goals. This score is significantly higher than both the Dutch (67) and Finnish (38) scores, suggesting that Jan is more focused on long-term success and sustainability than his peers in these cultures.

This long-term orientation likely influenced his strategic decisions throughout his career, such as his commitment to creating inclusive environments and fostering growth through mentoring but could have provided a backlash in terms of his planning not being perceived as detailed and actionable enough.

Indulgence vs. Restraint (IVR)

Jan's score of 48 in Indulgence indicates a balanced approach to enjoying life and exercising self-control. This score is somewhat aligned with the Dutch, Americans (68) and Belgian and Finnish (57) scores, suggesting that Jan values both leisure and discipline. The relatively small gaps imply that Jan has been able to adapt to the cultural norms of these countries, balancing work and life effectively.

Overall Reflection

Jan's cultural scores reveal a complex interplay between his personal values and the cultural environments of the Netherlands, Finland, the USA, and Belgium. His blindspots, such as a preference for high-Power Distance and Long-Term Orientation scores suggest that he values hierarchy and future planning, which may have set him apart in more egalitarian and short-term focused cultures like the Netherlands, USA and Finland, leaving his subordinates to become impatient and go over his head. Given the similarity expected with those cultures, blind spots are the things to look out for.

His steppingstones in relation to the cultures in his story were the relatively high focus on task execution (individualism) and similar level of indulgence.

However, even in these potential areas of alignment, there can be exceptions. For instance, in his experience in the USA, while individualism is generally valued, regional differences—such as the strong influence of religion on social connections (common in more short-term oriented cultures)—may overshadow the individualistic cultural alignment

His low Uncertainty Avoidance score indicates comfort with ambiguity and change, which likely helped him adapt to various challenging situations and diverse environments.

Story 2: Navigating Identity and Work in a Global Context

From the North of Europe to China - in this story we follow the journey of Anni, who grew up speaking a minority language in Finland, before coming back to Finland having experienced the world. Anni was born in the early '70s, with two siblings and grew up in Turku, a touristic city in Southern Finland.

Early Life in Turku and China

Anni grew up in a fully Swedish-speaking family in the heart of Turku. Her parents made no effort to introduce Finnish to her, resulting in her having no systematic exposure to the language until high school. This made her early interactions outside her home feel strange and challenging. At the age of 11,

Anni moved to China, where she attended a Swedish school with children from 15 different countries, all with parents working for multinational companies. As Anni mentioned in our interview,

"The school created a unique sense of being both an insider and an outsider. I spoke Swedish, but didn't quite feel like I belonged there."

First Encounter with "Foreignerness"

Anni vividly recalls feeling like a foreigner for the first time at the age of 8 when she felt nervous about purchasing things and was told to "go back to Sweden." Reaching out to other kids to play required a conscious effort, as she didn't know Finnish. Her father, who was bilingual, offered some support, but the experience marked the beginning of her awareness of cultural differences.

Starting Work Life in International Settings

Anni's professional journey has always been rooted in international environments. Her first jobs were in retail, but she quickly moved into more managerial roles. She began as a marketing and tourism coordinator, where she worked in a trilingual setting. This role was followed by positions in the USA and New Zealand before joining a bilateral chamber of commerce and eventually moving into the scale-up scene. Today, she works for a Spanish company covering three Nordic countries.

Working in such diverse environments has made Anni accustomed to feeling slightly uncomfortable, a state she has learned to navigate and embrace. This discomfort has driven her to make a conscious effort to ensure others feel included and at ease, developing a higher tolerance for different accents and cultural nuances.

Experiences of Onboarding

Anni's onboarding experiences across various organizations have been inconsistent. At the tourism agency, she started as an intern, which involved an ongoing dialogue that eased her transition. In contrast, other roles lacked proper onboarding, prompting her to create onboarding processes herself. For instance, in the US, conference onboarding included specific training on disability and staff adaptation. At a startup organization for foreigners, her manager was very inclusive, focusing on individuals' backgrounds and conducting regular check-ins. Monthly polls and eNPS surveys were part of the process to ensure everyone felt included.

At her current company, a professional services

provider, mandatory training, including inclusivity training, is provided, reflecting a structured approach to onboarding and continuous learning.

Encountering "Foreignerness" in Work life

Anni has frequently encountered "foreignerness" in her work life. One scenario involved working with colleagues from diverse cultural backgrounds, including Nordics, Filipinos, and Chinese. Despite the shared cultural context in her school in China, working with these different cultures presented challenges and learning opportunities.

A notable example of encountering "foreignerness" was with Russian and Ukrainian colleagues. Despite initial assumptions of cultural understanding, Anni found these interactions surprising and educational. She realized that cultures perceived as similar could still hold significant differences. Anni learned to navigate these differences by asking more questions and fostering a sense of camaraderie rather than trying to break down cultural walls.

Managing Cultural Differences

Anni's work experiences in North America significantly shaped her professional approach. After working for North American companies for six years, she consciously decided to move to a European culture, seeking more diversity. This shift aligned with her North American value profile but included Finnish work-life expectations.

One cultural clash involved a CEO attempting to apply US management styles, seen to be unwelcome micromanagement to the Nordic employees. Anni's insight helped the CEO understand that the US approach would not work in the Nordics, emphasising the need for cultural adaptability.

Another challenge was integrating employees from vastly different cultural backgrounds who struggled with the Finnish sense of personal responsibility and work-life balance. Anni worked on bridging these gaps, helping employees immerse themselves in the local culture while accommodating societal norms.

Reflecting on Personal and Professional Growth

Anni's journey from Turku to China, and her subsequent global career, has been a continuous process of learning and adaptation. Her early experiences of feeling different, her varied work environments, and her conscious efforts to create inclusive spaces have shaped her into a culturally sensitive and adaptable leader.

Reflecting on her journey, Anni continues to advocate for structured onboarding, cultural sensitivity, and inclusive practices in all her professional endeavours, ensuring that every individual feels valued and supported.

Understanding of a journey

Scores of selected countries based around the time of her movements.

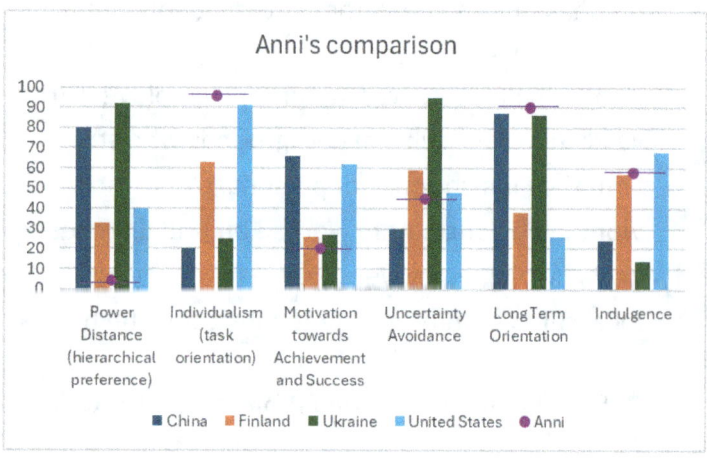

Reflection on Anni's Culture Scores

Anni's journey from Turku to China and her subsequent global career offers a fascinating context for interpreting her cultural scores. By examining Anni's Culture Compass scores and comparing them to the cultural values of the countries she has interacted with, we can gain deeper insights into how these cultural dynamics have shaped her experiences and challenges.

Power Distance (PDI)

Anni's score of 4 in Power Distance is exceptionally low, reflecting a strong preference for equality and an aversion to hierarchical structures. This score is much lower than the scores of countries like China (80) and the United States (40).

The significant gap with China, where Anni spent part of her childhood, suggests that she may have felt uncomfortable or even alienated in environments with rigid hierarchies and power imbalances. In contrast, the smaller gap with Finland (33), where Power Distance is also relatively low, likely contributed to her comfort and sense of belonging when she returned to her home country despite some challenges likely to occur. Anni's preference for egalitarian relationships likely influenced her leadership style and her approach to fostering inclusivity in the workplace.

Individualism (IDV)

With a score of 96 in Individualism, Anni exhibits a strong orientation towards personal independence and self-expression. Anni's high Individualism score suggests that she values autonomy, which aligns well with the cultural norms of Finland and especially the United States. However, the significant gap with China (20) and Ukraine (25), which are more collectivist, may have posed challenges for Anni when working in those environments. These differences likely required her to navigate cultural expectations carefully, balancing her individualistic tendencies with the collective orientation of her colleagues.

Assertiveness (MAS)

Anni's score of 20 in assertiveness reflects a preference for modesty, cooperation, and quality of life over competitiveness and assertiveness. This score is significantly lower than the American (62) and Chinese (66) values.

These substantial differences suggest that Anni may have found the competitive, achievement-driven cultures of the United States and China challenging. Her lower assertiveness score aligns more closely with the cultures of Finland (26) and Ukraine (27), where similar values of modesty and work-life balance are emphasised. This alignment likely contributed to Anni's decision to return to Europe and work in environments where cooperation and inclusivity are prioritised.

Uncertainty Avoidance (UAI)

Anni's score of 45 in Uncertainty Avoidance indicates a moderate level of comfort with ambiguity and a preference for flexibility, almost a perfect match with American (48) values and rather close to Chinese (30) and Finnish (59) values. However, the significant gaps with Ukraine (95) - in the opposite direction - suggests that Anni may have faced challenges there. Her moderate score likely made her adaptable to various cultural contexts, but it also required her to navigate different attitudes towards risk and uncertainty carefully.

Long-Term Orientation (LTO)

Anni's score of 90 in Long-Term Orientation reflects a strong focus on future planning, perseverance, and long-term goals. This score is significantly higher than both the Finnish (38) and American (26) values, which suggests that Anni's approach to planning and goal setting may have been more future-oriented than the typical Finnish and American preference for quarterly results. This focus on long-term goals likely influenced her career decisions and her ability to adapt to different cultural environments. The very small gap with China (87) may have contributed to her ability to navigate the cultural differences she encountered during her time there.

Indulgence (IVR)

Anni's score of 58 in Indulgence indicates a balanced approach to enjoying life and embracing personal freedom. This score is relatively aligned with the American (68) and Finnish (57) values. The relatively small gaps suggest that Anni values leisure and personal fulfilment but may be less impulsive compared to her American counterparts. This balanced approach likely helped her adapt to various cultural contexts, including those with lower Indulgence scores like China (24), where self-restraint and discipline are more emphasised.

Overall Reflection

When reflecting on Anni's cultural scores and comparing them to the values of Finnish, American, Chinese, and Ukraine, it becomes clear that her personal values often align closely with those of Finland, while also reflecting significant differences from other cultures she has interacted with.

Anni's low Power Distance, high Individualism, and strong Long-Term Orientation suggest that she values equality, autonomy, and future planning—traits that have shaped her approach to leadership and her efforts to create inclusive, forward-thinking work environments.

However, the significant gaps in assertiveness and Indulgence indicate that Anni may have found certain aspects of American and Chinese culture challenging, particularly their emphasis on competitiveness and lack of work-life focus.

Story 3 - Team Building Challenges at Teravamuoti

In the next story, we reflect on the journey of Kalle, a man in his forties, who grew up in Kuopio, Finland in a typical family house in a quiet neighbourhood with his parents and a sister who is 5 years younger. Kalle reflects on the hard lessons learned when reflecting on becoming foreign to one's own self perceptions and the actions needed to adjust.

Early Life and Personal Development

In the house where Kalle grew up, the focus was primarily on work and sports, typical for a post-2nd World War family, with emotional skills being somewhat limited. It took Kalle time and self-development to realise the importance of emotional intelligence. His first significant realisation came with his first wife and the mother of his sons. Reflecting on the differences between his emotionally reserved family and his wife's more expressive one, Kalle learned about the importance of addressing emotions and handling reactions in conflict situations. As Kalle mentioned,

> *"In my family, we didn't really talk about emotions, we expressed feelings in behaviour, simply ploughing through tough times without really ever taking the time to understand our emotions."*

The Wake-Up Call

A major turning point for Kalle came during counselling therapy, where he gained a deeper understanding of his capabilities and how his behaviour impacted others.

He reflected on how his behaviour changed in the presence of his ex-wife (fearful and subdued) versus when she was absent (happy and relaxed). This insight spurred continuous self-development and a commitment to improving his emotional intelligence.

Leadership Challenges at Teravamuoti

As the CEO of Teravamuoti, Kalle faced significant

team-building issues. The current Chairman exhibited aggressive behaviour, including publicly throwing employees "under the bus."

This triggered Kalle's childhood behaviour of not being able to react on the spot, reminiscent of the fearful boy he once was. Recognizing the need to draw a line, Kalle sought to activate his leadership skills and address these challenges head-on.

Handling Emotional and Conflict Situations

Kalle implemented strategies to manage emotions and conflicts at work. One positive approach was to hold discussions when emotions ran high: *"We created a pause to pick a better time for conversations."*

However, managing this in a group setting proved challenging. While there were intentions to talk about values, equality, and behaviour, the lack of active guidance meant these good intentions didn't always translate into practical actions.

Navigating Cultural Differences and Conflict

Teravamuoti provided practical support for non-Finnish employees settling in Finland. With the onset of the Ukraine war, extra attention was paid to the feelings of Russian employees, leading to the removal of national flags from the office to maintain neutrality.

However, ongoing conflicts between US and Finnish approaches to work-life balance emerged. The shift towards a more US-centric way of working created friction, undermining the "one team" approach and causing information flow issues.

This passive-aggressive transformation led to the departure of old leadership and a reluctance to participate in bilateral management meetings.

The Impact of Investment and Leadership Division

Two years ago, a major US investor made a $20 million investment in Teravamuoti, largely due to Kalle's efforts as CEO. Since then, significant changes have occurred, leading to divided opinions between the US and Europe.

The differing perspectives on reporting reality versus selling a dream caused tension. Classic American values, such as High individualism (IDV) and assertiveness (MAS), combined with low long-term orientation (LTO), led to delayed truth-telling, resulting in public yelling and a toxic work environment at the senior leadership level as the overall style was counter to the less assertive and more holistic European style. This created a complete lack of trust and constant second-guessing of motivations.

Building a Cohesive Team

Kalle believes that being in the physical office and having open communication helps counter the feeling of foreignerness and keeps everyone on the same page. He emphasises the importance of open communication to foster a sense of unity and shared understanding among the team.

Conclusion: Navigating Leadership and Cultural Challenges

Kalle's journey as the CEO of Teravamuoti highlights the importance of emotional intelligence, open communication, and cultural sensitivity in leadership.

By addressing team-building issues head-on and fostering a supportive environment, Kalle aims to create a cohesive and inclusive workplace. His experiences underscore the need for continuous self-development and the value of understanding and adapting to different cultural contexts in achieving effective leadership.

Understanding of a journey

Scores of selected countries based around the time of his movements.

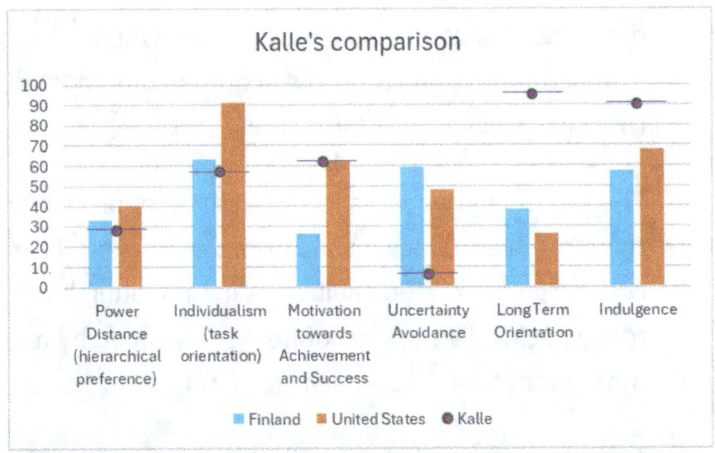

Reflection on Kalle's Culture Scores

Kalle's journey as the CEO of Teravamuoti not only highlights the complexities of leadership in a multicultural environment but also reflects the deeper cultural dynamics at play.

By examining Kalle's Culture Compass scores and comparing them to the values of Finnish culture and the USA, we can gain further insight into his experiences and the challenges he faced.

Power Distance (PDI)

Kalle's score of 28 in Power Distance indicates a

preference for equality and a low tolerance for hierarchical structures.

This aligns closely with Finnish culture, which also values low power distance (33). However, the differences became more pronounced when interacting with cultures that scored higher in Power Distance, such as the United States (40).

The friction between Kalle's egalitarian approach and the more hierarchical expectations of his American counterparts created challenges in his leadership role, specifically because of being reinforced by his more team based approach (see IDV).

This cultural gap likely contributed to the difficulties he faced in managing the team, as he struggled to balance his own leadership style with the expectations of others.

Individualism (IDV)

Kalle's score of 57 in Individualism reflects a moderate level of individualistic values, which is somewhat lower than the typical Finnish score (63). This indicates that Kalle may value group cohesion and collaboration more than the average Finn, which aligns with his efforts to foster a team-oriented environment at Teravamuoti.

However, when compared to the United States, which scored 91, Kalle's lower emphasis on individualism might have made it challenging for him to fully align with the more individualistic American mindset.

This difference in cultural orientation could explain some of the conflicts between the Finnish and US teams, particularly around issues of autonomy.

Assertiveness (MAS)

With a score of 62 in assertiveness, Kalle leans towards a competitive and achievement-oriented mindset, higher than the Finnish average (26). This difference suggests that Kalle might have been more driven by success and recognition than his Finnish peers, possibly leading to internal conflicts when trying to implement changes.

However, in comparison to the US culture, where the score is 66, Kalle's score is more closely aligned, indicating that he may have found common ground with the American team in terms of striving for excellence and results, though his focus was likely on team achievements rather than individual achievements, as Kalle's preference on Individualism was 57.

Uncertainty Avoidance (UAI)

Kalle's extremely low score of 6 in Uncertainty Avoidance suggests a high tolerance for ambiguity and change, which is in stark contrast to the Finnish culture, which scores 59. This significant gap indicates that Kalle was more comfortable with risk-taking and navigating uncertain situations than his Finnish colleagues, who may have preferred stability and clear guidelines.

This difference might have made Kalle's leadership style appear unconventional or even risky to others within the organisation, particularly during times of change or crisis, when people would prefer more predictable approaches.

Long-Term Orientation (LTO)

Kalle's score of 95 in Long-Term Orientation is strikingly high, especially when compared to the American (26) and Finnish score (38). This score suggests that Kalle is highly future-oriented, with a strong focus on long-term planning and perseverance.

This orientation likely influenced his strategic decisions at Teravamuoti, driving him to prioritise sustainable growth and long-term goals over short-term gains. However, this focus may have been challenging to communicate to teams that were more concerned with immediate results, particularly in the United States, where the score is significantly lower at 26.

Indulgence (IVR)

Finally, Kalle's score of 90 in Indulgence indicates a strong inclination towards enjoying life and embracing personal freedom, much higher than the Finnish (57) and USA (68) averages. This suggests that Kalle values a work-life balance and personal well-being, which could have influenced his approach to managing the team and fostering a positive workplace culture. However, this value might have clashed with the more restrained and disciplined attitudes of others within the organisation, particularly those who were more focused on work-centric goals.

Overall Reflection

When reflecting on Kalle's cultural scores and comparing them to the Finnish and American values, it becomes clear that the challenges he faced at Teravamuoti were deeply rooted in cultural differences. His low Power Distance and Uncertainty Avoidance, combined with a high Long-Term Orientation and Indulgence, positioned him as a leader who valued equality, risk-taking, and future planning. However, these traits were not always in harmony with the expectations of his team members, particularly those from the United States.

Another important observation from Kalle's story is the transition he went through during his marriage. In families where the overall focus is on ignoring emotions, even in more consensus-oriented societies (low MAS), people will display significantly more output oriented focus (high MAS).

When life gets tough (e.g., through lack of sleep, highly stressful jobs), this inability to understand emotions due to a lack of being taught a language of how to deal with them, can create strong emotional internal conflicts which will find their way into work life.

In our latest research at The Culture Factor Group, we can see clear generational differences between generations dubbed "millenials" and "Gen Z" and their need for more emotion-based discussions compared to how most managers have been educated by traditional MBA's, with most managers also coming from the generation dubbed "Gen X".

For more about these insights you can read here: https://www.theculturefactor.com/resources/report/global-report-2024

Story 4 From Florida to Finland – The Eastern route

In a time of rapid change with the fall of the Berlin Wall, Eastern Europe opened up again. In this story, we encounter how new opportunities arose for both West and East through the experience of Adrian, who left the USA in his early 20s during this period of profound social change in Europe during the early '90s. Adrian grew up in Tallahassee, Florida (United States) in a typical family with both his parents and a younger sister.

Early Years in Florida

Growing up in Florida, Adrian's first eight or nine years were marked by constant change and movement. His father, a Southern human rights activist journalist, likely planted the seeds of Adrian's curiosity about the world and a passion for equality. His father's work inspired him, but Adrian chose not to follow in his professional footsteps. Instead, he developed a keen interest in education, driven by a desire to help people take advantage of their new opportunities.

As a child, Adrian often moved from one school to another, which made it difficult to settle in and form lasting friendships. Perhaps what made him stand out the most during these years was his preference for soccer over the more popular American football. This choice, along with his frequent relocations, contributed to a sense of foreignerness to his peers.

Post-Wall Central Europe

After graduating, Adrian decided to move to Central Europe, a region undergoing significant changes during the post-Communist years. His first job was as an English teacher in Czechoslovakia. On his first day at school, the headmaster welcomed him by opening a booze cabinet, setting the tone for the warm and inclusive interactions he would experience throughout his time there. At the age of 22, he felt a genuine sense of belonging, whether at school, with colleagues, or in the local shops.

In the town where Adrian taught, he was recognized and appreciated as "our teacher." This recognition and the frequent invitations to social gatherings provided a strong sense of community and positive feedback, contributing to a "feel-good factor" that enriched his experience in Czechoslovakia.

Adventures in Central Europe

Adrian's journey then took him to Bratislava, Slovakia, and later to Hungary, where he spent eight formative years. Each move brought new challenges and opportunities to integrate into different cultures. In Hungary, he worked at a language school in Budapest where the atmosphere was one of camaraderie and mutual support. The feeling that "we are all in this together" permeated the workplace, and he felt genuinely appreciated by the school's owners.

The school fostered a sense of community through numerous parties and anniversaries that included both employees and customers. This openness extended to the school's operations, with frequent updates on its performance and ample opportunities for learning and growth. The sense of belonging and appreciation Adrian felt during his time in Budapest left a lasting impression on him.

A Journey Through Poland and the Czech Republic

After Hungary, Adrian's journey continued to Poland and then to what had become the Czech Republic. Each move brought new experiences and insights into the diverse cultures of Central Europe. He cherished the moments of connection and the opportunities to learn from different perspectives. The sense of being a foreigner in these countries was tempered by the warmth and hospitality of the people he encountered.

Settling in Finland

For the past 23 years, Adrian has made Finland his home. Here, he married a woman who is half-Czech, and together they built a life in a country that offers stability and predictability. Finland, with its less extreme social and cultural dynamics, provided a contrast to the more volatile environments he had experienced in Central Europe.

Reflecting on his journey, Adrian realised that each country offered unique lessons and opportunities for growth. Finland's culture, while less surprising, provided a solid foundation for building a family and a career. The experiences of moving and adapting to different environments shaped his worldview and deepened his appreciation for diversity. In our interview Adrian reflected on his journey and when asked about which culture he identifies with most, his answer was *"I am very much an American, but…"*

Reflections on Work Life

Looking back on his work life, the years Adrian spent at the language school in Budapest stand out as particularly impactful. The collaborative atmosphere and the genuine appreciation from both colleagues and the school's owners created a supportive and enriching environment. The openness about the school's performance and the opportunities for learning fostered a culture of growth and inclusion.

This experience taught Adrian the importance of feeling valued and included in the workplace. It highlighted the significance of community and support in achieving professional and personal fulfilment. These lessons continue to influence his approach to work and relationships today.

Understanding of a journey

Scores of selected countries based around the time of his movements.

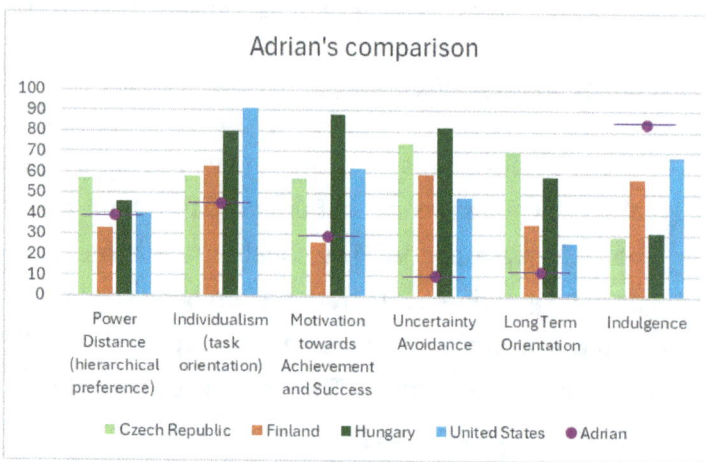

As Adrian mentioned in his story, he identifies as American. Compared with the four countries he spent a lot of time in, his gap is smallest when compared with the USA.

Reflection on Adrian's Culture Scores

Adrian's journey from the United States to various parts of Central Europe, and eventually settling in Finland, provides a rich context for interpreting his cultural scores.

By examining Adrian's Culture Compass scores and comparing them to the values of the cultures he interacted with, we gain deeper insights into his experiences and the cultural challenges he navigated.

Power Distance (PDI)

Adrian's score of 39 in Power Distance reflects a moderate preference for equality and a relatively low tolerance for hierarchical structures. This score closely aligns with both Finnish (33), American (40) and Hungarian (46) values. This alignment suggests that Adrian is comfortable in environments where authority is decentralised and where there is a significant degree of equality in interpersonal relationships. However, when interacting with cultures with higher Power Distance, such as the Czech Republic (57), Adrian may have experienced some discomfort or difficulty adapting to more hierarchical settings.

Individualism (IDV)

Adrian's score of 45 in Individualism is notably lower than both the Finnish (63) and American (91) scores, indicating a more collective orientation compared to these cultures. The gaps could explain the stronger affinity for the community-oriented environments he found in Central Europe. However, he may have gravitated towards organisations, like the Hungarian language school, whose management style was more collectivist than the national norms.

Assertiveness (MAS)

With a score of 29 in assertiveness, Adrian displays a preference for modesty, care for others, and quality of life over competitiveness and assertiveness. This score is lower than American (66) values, indicating that Adrian leans towards more cooperative and nurturing interactions. The small gap with Finland (3 points) suggests that Adrian found a cultural fit in Finnish society, which also values consensus and modesty. In contrast, the significant gap with the United States (40 points) and even larger gaps with more assertive cultures like Hungary (59 points) may have made Adrian feel out of place in more competitive or achievement-driven environments.

This difference could explain his preference for workplaces that foster community and mutual support, as seen in his perhaps surprisingly positive experiences in Hungary.

Uncertainty Avoidance (UAI)

Adrian's score of 10 in Uncertainty Avoidance is extremely low, indicating a high tolerance for ambiguity and a preference for flexibility and spontaneity. This attitude contrasts sharply with Finland (59) and Hungary (82), where there is a much stronger desire for predictability and clear rules.

Adrian's low score suggests that he thrives in environments where adaptability is key, which likely helped him navigate the various transitions in his life, from moving to post-Communist Central Europe to settling in Finland. However, this trait may have also led to challenges in more structured environments, where others may have preferred stability and clear guidelines.

Long-Term Orientation (LTO)

Adrian's score of 12 in Long-Term Orientation reflects a strong preference for short-term goals and traditions over long-term planning and perseverance. This score is significantly lower than the Czech (70) and Hungarian (58) values which value longer term planning and sustainability.

However, in environments like the United States and Finland, where short-term results are often emphasised, Adrian's orientation may have been more compatible.

Indulgence (IVR)

Adrian's score of 84 in Indulgence is very high, indicating a strong inclination towards enjoying life and embracing personal freedom, even more strongly so than the closed national culture scores such as the American (68) and Finnish (57) scores.

This orientation towards indulgence likely contributed to his positive experiences in various countries, as he sought out and appreciated the opportunities for personal growth and enjoyment in each new environment, looking for the positive. Despite the more restrained cultural nature of, for example, the Czech Republic or Hungary, the organizations where he worked ensured sufficient optimism and indulgence to meet his needs.

Overall Reflection

When reflecting on Adrian's cultural scores and comparing them to the values of Finnish, American, and Central European cultures, it becomes clear that his personal values often align closely with those of Finland and the United States. Adrian's low Power Distance, low Uncertainty Avoidance, and high Indulgence scores suggest that he values equality, adaptability, and the enjoyment of life—traits that helped him navigate the diverse and rapidly changing environments of Central and Eastern Europe.

However, the significant gaps in Individualism and Long-Term Orientation indicate that Adrian may have felt out of sync with certain aspects of Finnish and American culture, particularly their emphasis on individual achievement and short-term planning.

Story 5 – Navigating Leadership and Communication in a Global Context

In this chapter, we fly along with John, a South African pilot, who has worked across Africa, the Middle East and Canada.

John is a former fighter pilot in his late forties, and flying instructor with a Masters degree in Aviation Management from Australia, formerly married to a Canadian and Australian.

He spent 20 years as an aviation trainer and manager in the Arabian peninsula, Canada and Australia, and worked as culture consultant and coach at large multinationals and with individual clients from all over the world. Currently, he is a training manager at the Qantas Group Pilot Academy in Queensland, Australia. John grew up in Bloemfontein, South Africa, with white Afrikaans-speaking South African parents from Dutch descent and he is the oldest of three siblings.

Discovering the Shadow Self

"The concept of shadow work, as phrased by Carl Jung (MBTI), plays a significant role in understanding one's deeper self," says John, an extraverted leader, who used external coaching to shine a light on his own inner workings, reflecting on his perception and actions.

This journey into the shadow self, allowed him to understand and transcend cultural boundaries by establishing a personal code of honesty, responsibility, and quality, especially during his time as an expat in the Middle East region.

He learned to live up to his own standards rather than following local expectations, creating a strong foundation for his leadership.

A Lesson in Communication

John's experiences in aviation provide a rich ground for understanding cultural nuances and communication challenges. One notable instance involved a South African co-pilot and a Japanese captain flying for a Japanese Cargo company as John described in our interview.

"So, the captain and co-pilot had minimal interaction, with a significant communication gap throughout a ten-hour flight, barely uttering a "hello" and "checklist completed" upon starting their flight, and a "goodbye, have a nice stay" in the end of the flight, imagine having to be silent that long."

This scenario highlighted the cultural differences in communication styles and the need for awareness and adaptation.

If the co-pilot would have been Finnish, the silence most likely would not have been any issue, giving a nice example of how understanding cultural differences can help to alleviate unnecessary stress involving "awkward" silences.

Another example was an American student's interaction during a briefing on emergency procedures.

The student's seemingly cavalier attitude towards an engine fire warning contrasted sharply with the more structured and cautious approach expected by the instructor. This incident underscored the perception of Americans as "cowboys" and the importance of precise communication in critical situations.

Navigating Language Barriers

John encountered significant challenges in the Arabic-speaking world, particularly in Kuwait. An engine problem required the shutdown of a fuel pump, but confusion arose due to the Arabic terms for "on/off" being the same as "open/close." This linguistic nuance led to immense confusion, emphasising the need for agreed terminology in multilingual settings.

Another story involved an airbrake incident where an instructor's command to "break out" (something he thought was universally understood by pilots) was misinterpreted by a student as "pull the airbrake." This mistake caused the aircraft to dive deep through the skyline of Riyadh, teaching John the critical lesson of precise wording and the potential consequences of miscommunication.

Reflecting on Cultural Interactions

John's early exposure to different cultures began at a young age in South Africa. Growing up with an Xhosa nanny, Zulu gardener, and other domestic help, he observed how white households communicated differently with those who looked different. This experience taught him to adjust his communication style to suit various cultural contexts, a skill that proved invaluable in Arab cultures.

British and Australian colleagues often struggled with cultural adaptation, displaying a lack of sympathy. However, John's approach as a key instructor emphasised continuous learning for the instructors themselves.

By encouraging them to engage in new activities like painting or paragliding, he helped them realise the challenges and perspectives of being a learner, fostering empathy and better communication skills.

The Importance of "Parsimony"

One of John's significant realisations was the complexity of the English language and the confusion it can cause for non-native speakers. The concept of "parsimony" (being scarce with words) became essential in his communication, teaching him to be more deliberate and clearer in his instructions. This awareness of linguistic intricacies helped him bridge cultural gaps and improve interactions with diverse teams.

Cultivating a Learning Environment

John's experiences highlight the importance of fostering a learning environment for leaders and instructors.

By continuously engaging in new activities and understanding the learner's perspective, he and his colleagues developed greater empathy and communication skills.

This approach not only improved their effectiveness as instructors but also created a more inclusive and supportive atmosphere for everyone involved.

Reflecting on his journey, John continues to advocate for clear communication, cultural sensitivity, and continuous learning in all his professional endeavours. His story underscores the value of understanding and adapting to cultural differences, creating a more harmonious and effective work environment.

Understanding of a journey

Scores of selected countries based around the time of his movements.

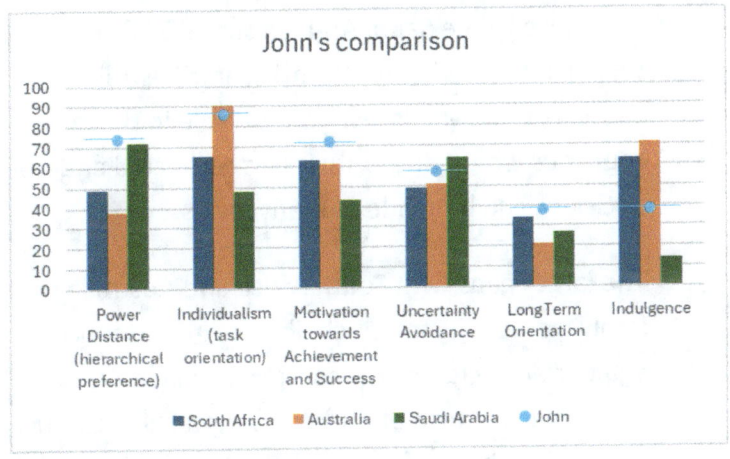

Reflection on John's Culture Scores

John's journey from South Africa across the Middle East, Australia, and Canada provides an intriguing context for understanding how his cultural values shaped his leadership and communication style.

By examining John's Culture Compass scores and comparing them to the values of the countries he has lived and worked in, we can gain deeper insights into how these cultural dynamics influenced his experiences and challenges.

Power Distance Index (PDI)

John's score of 74 in Power Distance indicates a relatively high tolerance for hierarchical structures and authority. This score is higher than both the South African (49) and Australian (38) scores, but very close to the Saudi Arabian score (72). The significant gap with South Africa and Australia suggests that John is less comfortable in those countries where authority is less respected and decisions can be made at many levels.

The larger gaps with South Africa and Australia could imply initial adjustment challenges in these more egalitarian societies. His comfort level with the hierarchical nature of Middle Eastern cultures, such as Saudi Arabia, may have contributed to his success there.

Individualism vs. Collectivism (IDV)

John's score of 86 in Individualism reflects a strong emphasis on personal autonomy and self-expression. This score is fairly close to the original Individualism score for South Africa (65) as that was based on the scores of the white South African population, yet significantly higher than the current South African score (23) which incorporates values from across South Africa.

His score is much higher than the Saudi Arabian score (48). The large gap indicates that John highly values individual achievement and freedom, which might have clashed with the more collectivist cultures he encountered in South Africa and Saudi Arabia, where group harmony and family loyalty are prioritised. In contrast, his score aligns more closely with Australia (73), a country that also emphasises individualism. This alignment may have facilitated his adaptation to Australian culture, where his individualistic tendencies could flourish.

Assertiveness (MAS)

With a score of 72 in assertiveness, John exhibits a strong focus on competition, achievement, and success. This score is slightly higher than the South African (63) and Australian (61) scores, but significantly higher than the Saudi Arabian score (43). The relatively small gap with South Africa and Australia likely helped him fit in professionally. However, the larger gap with Saudi Arabia, which values modesty and cooperation, might have posed challenges when navigating the cultural expectations there, requiring him to adjust his leadership style to foster more collaborative and nurturing environments.

Uncertainty Avoidance Index (UAI)

John's score of 57 in Uncertainty Avoidance suggests a moderate level of comfort with ambiguity and risk-taking. This score is somewhat aligned with the Saudi Arabian (64), South African (49) and Australian (51) scores, indicating that John felt comfortable with the uncertainty and ambiguity inherent in these cultures.

Long-Term Orientation vs. Short-Term Normative Orientation (LTO)

John's score of 38 in Long-Term Orientation reflects a balanced focus on both short-term and long-term goals, with a slight preference for traditions and maintaining established norms compared to more long-term oriented cultures.

His reflection on parsimony indicates that John realised that in more short-term oriented cultures, such as South Africa (34), Australia (21) and Saudi Arabia (14), he needs to be more to the point and more literal in the words he chooses to use.

Indulgence vs. Restraint (IVR)

John's score of 38 in Indulgence indicates a tendency towards restraint and self-control. The gaps with South Africa (63) and Australia (71) suggest that John may have found it challenging to adapt to cultures that value leisure, enjoyment, and a more relaxed approach to life.

Conversely, his lower Indulgence score aligns more closely with Saudi Arabian (14) values, where restraint, modesty, and self-discipline are emphasised. This alignment likely aided his adaptation in the more conservative cultural environment of Saudi Arabia.

Overall Reflection

John's cultural scores reveal a nuanced balance between his personal values and the diverse cultural environments of South Africa, Australia, and Saudi Arabia. His high scores in Power Distance and Individualism suggest a preference for structured authority and personal autonomy, which may have positioned him well in hierarchical and individualistic cultures, such as Saudi Arabia and Australia and in general his career in the military.

However, the significant gaps with South African and Australian scores in areas like Indulgence and Assertiveness indicate that John may have experienced periods of cultural tension or adjustment, particularly in navigating less competitive or more indulgent settings.

Story 6 Navigating Identity and Career in Post-War Bosnia-Herzegovina

What happens to our sense of national identity when our country formally ceases to exist? How does it impact on how we view ourselves and those around us? In the following story, we follow Dino, in his journey through post-war former Yugoslavia. Dino grew up in Foca, a small town in what is today eastern Bosnia, before moving to Sarajevo in a family with both parents as teachers and one older brother, who is eight years older.

Early Life in Yugoslavia and War-Torn Bosnia

Growing up in Yugoslavia, Dino's early years were spent in a communist environment that, while restrictive, was somewhat more open compared to other Eastern European countries.

He lived in Sarajevo from ages 12 to 16, a pivotal period that coincided with the Bosnian War. During the war, the country was engulfed in fierce patriotic fervour. However, post-war Bosnia transformed into a new entity, and the intense patriotic feelings dissipated. This new Bosnia made Dino feel more connected to the city and its local identity.

Education and Early Career

Dino's education in the 1990s was deeply rooted in local institutions. He studied computer engineering at a local academy and began his career working in a bank. This period was marked by a stark transition from the wartime environment where clear distinctions between friends and enemies existed to a post-war context where these lines blurred.

During the war, material possessions like the size of one's house were irrelevant, and this perception changed in the post-war era as Bosnia grappled with a corrupted version of capitalism, leading to a growing disconnect with the country and more focus on the individual/regional context, as Dino reflected on it

"I just did not feel any connection with the country, it was more about your local neighbourhood, at most the city itself."

The Banking Industry and Corporate Mergers

Dino's early professional life was shaped by significant changes in the banking sector. The local bank he worked for was acquired by an Austrian bank. This merger experience was disorienting as he felt his ways were being pushed out in favour of new, unfamiliar practices.

The advice to "not push, just give in" during the merger left a lasting impression. Surviving another merger with an Italian bank reinforced the feeling of being marginalised, especially in the IT department, which was always seen as a cost centre rather than as a source of profit.

Transition to An American software company

Joining an American software company marked a significant shift in Dino's career and exposure. The contrast between the formal, rigid banking environment and the more relaxed, results-oriented culture at the American software company was stark.

At the bank, punctuality and a tidy desk were paramount, whereas at the American software company, the focus was on getting the job done regardless of when or where.

His initial role in support at the American software company was eye-opening, with extensive training and a great deal of freedom. His former co-workers in the banking sector were in awe of his new job. The difference between cultures helped him understand the value of appreciation.

Onboarding and Early Impressions at an American software company

At the American software company's Academy, a three-week onboarding program, introduced Dino to all business units and was a full immersion into the company's culture. The dedication and resources available were beyond anything he had experienced in a typical Bosnian company.

Despite the opportunities at the American software company, career progression in a small market was slower, requiring exposure to various roles to ensure he was able to make enough of a name for himself and as such open opportunities.

Evolving Roles and Team Dynamics

Dino's career at the American software company evolved from local support to regional and then to a global team over the past eight years. Although he often felt like an outsider in his IT support role, the continuous communication within the team maintained strong bonds.

The discontinuation of the American software company's Academy impacted the overall perception of investment in employees. The strong alumni feeling that once existed has diminished, particularly with remote work becoming more prevalent and as such, the sense of belonging has weakened, although efforts to create team cohesion through offsites and other initiatives have shown positive results.

When Dino grew as a Technical Account Manager, adjusting to the CxO level required managing accounts, selling, and delivering services. As such, extensive training on stakeholder management and soft sales skills was provided, offering ample learning opportunities. This role led Dino to discover a passion for change management.

Building Team Spirit and Customer Connection

Creating a sense of belonging has always been about fostering team spirit. In Bosnia, work often gets done over lunch or coffee, embodying a "work in the street" concept. During the COVID-19 pandemic, Dino volunteered to maintain physical connections with customers, emphasising the importance of personal interaction.

Leadership and Team Bonding

The American software company's "lone-wolf" approach sometimes hinders the feeling of belonging, although there has been a shift towards more team-oriented co-delivery based on pilots initiated by Dino. Good managers have played a crucial role in Dino's career. For instance, an Austrian manager's ability to separate work and personal life through heated discussions followed by a smoke break taught him valuable lessons. Despite cultural shocks, the team spirit has always been a source of motivation and strength.

Conclusion: Reflecting on a Journey of Change

Reflecting on his journey from war-torn Bosnia to a global career at the American software company, the importance of community, recognition, and team spirit stands out.

Each phase of Dino's life has been a testament to the power of adaptability and the value of supportive environments. As he continues to navigate his career, these experiences underscore the significance of fostering a sense of belonging and investing in personal and professional growth.

Understanding of a journey

Scores of selected countries from Dino's story

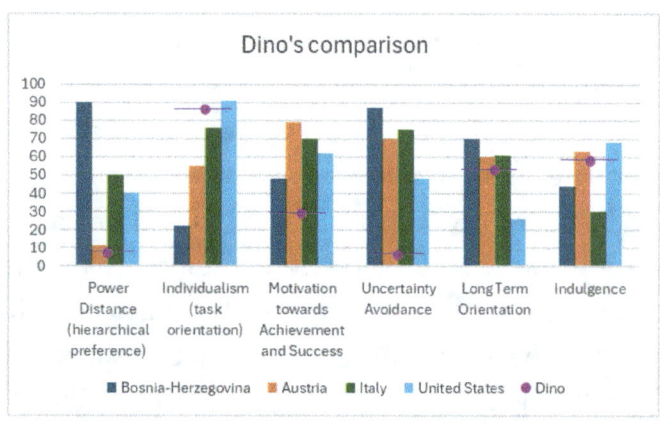

Reflection on Dino's Culture Scores

Dino's journey through post-war Bosnia, navigating the complexities of identity and career, provides a rich context for interpreting his cultural scores. By examining Dino's Culture Compass scores and comparing them to the values of Bosnian culture and other countries he has interacted with, we gain a deeper understanding of his experiences and the challenges he faced.

Power Distance (PDI)

Dino's score of 7 in Power Distance is exceptionally low, indicating a strong preference for equality and minimal hierarchy in relationships.

This score contrasts sharply with the traditional Bosnian culture, which scores much higher at 90. The significant gap of 83 points suggests that Dino often felt at odds with the hierarchical structures that dominated Bosnian society and workplaces. This difference likely contributed to his sense of alienation, particularly during corporate mergers where power dynamics were starkly pronounced.

Dino's preference for flat structures may have made it challenging for him to navigate environments where authority and status played a more prominent role.

Individualism (IDV)

With a high score of 86 in Individualism, Dino values personal independence and self-expression, which again diverges significantly from the Bosnian score of 40.

This could explain why Dino felt a growing disconnect in post-war Bosnia, as society became more focused on regional and individual identities rather than collective national identity. In his career, especially in the context of mergers and working within multinational companies, Dino's individualistic values may have clashed with the more collective or group-oriented approaches of his colleagues, particularly in environments that emphasised teamwork over individual achievement.

Assertiveness (MAS)

Dino's score of 29 in assertiveness reflects a relatively low emphasis on competitiveness, assertiveness and achievement. This is substantially below the Bosnian score of 48, indicating that while Bosnian culture may still value these traits, Dino personally leans towards a more cooperative and modest approach.

The gap between his score and that of the countries he interacted with, such as Austria (79) and Italy (70), might have made Dino feel out of place in more aggressive or achievement-driven environments. His preference for a less confrontational and more collaborative work style likely influenced his approach to leadership and team dynamics, as seen in his appreciation for strong team bonds and continuous communication.

Uncertainty Avoidance (UAI)

Dino's score of 6 in Uncertainty Avoidance is

remarkably low, suggesting that he is highly comfortable with ambiguity and uncertainty. This contrasts sharply with Bosnia's high score of 87, which indicates a preference for stability and clear rules.

The 81-point gap here reflects Dino's greater openness to change and innovation, which may have caused friction in environments where change and innovation were seen as threats.

Dino's tolerance for uncertainty likely helped him adapt to the rapidly changing post-war environment and navigate the unpredictable nature of corporate mergers. However, this same trait may have made him feel like an outsider in his home culture.

Long-Term Orientation (LTO)

Dino's score of 53 in Long-Term Orientation suggests a balanced approach between short-term and long-term planning. Compared to Bosnia's score of 36, Dino places a greater emphasis on future planning and perseverance, though the gap is not as large as in other dimensions.

This might explain his success in navigating the long-term impacts of corporate changes and his eventual focus on change management, where a strategic, future-oriented mindset is crucial. Dino's ability to think ahead likely helped him find his niche in change management, where he could leverage his skills in planning and adaptability to help organisations navigate complex transitions.

Indulgence (IVR)

Dino's score of 58, slightly higher than Bosnia's 44, in Indulgence indicates a moderate preference for enjoying life and embracing leisure activities. This value is reflected in his efforts to maintain strong team bonds and personal connections, particularly through informal interactions like coffee or lunch meetings.

Dino's moderate indulgence score may have helped him connect with colleagues in less formal settings, fostering a sense of belonging and community even in challenging corporate environments.

Overall Reflection

When reflecting on Dino's cultural scores and comparing them to Bosnian and other cultural values, it becomes evident that his personal values often diverged significantly from the dominant cultural norms in his home country.

Dino's low Power Distance and Uncertainty Avoidance scores, coupled with high Individualism, positioned him as someone who valued equality, independence, and adaptability. These traits likely helped him thrive in the diverse and rapidly changing environments of post-war Bosnia and multinational corporations.

However, these same cultural preferences also contributed to a sense of alienation and the feeling of being an outsider, both in his home country and in the corporate settings he navigated.

Story 7 Embracing Multiculturalism and Flexibility in Leadership

Building a strong sense of self by purposeful exposure to new languages describes the journey of Yevgeni in our next story.

Early Exposure to Multiculturalism

Yevgeni grew up in a multicultural environment in Strasbourg, exposed to different languages and cultures from a young age. His parents were young illegal immigrants from Yugoslavia, and they had to adopt a French name while speaking Serbian at home. This diverse background, combined with the touristy nature of Strasbourg, created a rich environment for Yevgeni to practise and experience different cultures.

However, he also encountered strong regional pride in the region of Alsace, which sometimes bordered on narrow-mindedness, as quoted from our interview

"People took so much pride in the region, that everything from outside the region was automatically considered bad, dumb, or arrogant."

In response, Yevgeni defied these limitations by learning new languages and immersing himself in various cultures through travel and professional opportunities.

Career and Cultural Adaptation

Yevgeni's career took him to the UK for ten years after his studies, where he faced a steep learning curve to fit into the local culture in the Midlands and up North.

Returning to France having over the years inherited a strong British accent presented its own challenges, requiring six months to readjust to French culture. His Eastern European background, combined with an

Anglo-Saxon professional experience in a Latin country, provided a unique perspective and adaptability.

Managing Multicultural Teams

Throughout his career, Yevgeni had the opportunity to manage highly multicultural teams. Over his career, he managed teams of up to 75 people from 18 different countries, spanning from Sydney to Seattle, Vietnam, New Zealand, Europe, and Brazil. This exposure to diverse cultures gave Yevgeni the flexibility to adjust his management style to suit his employees rather than imposing a standard playbook.

He learned to balance the needs and cultural nuances of his team members, understanding that a one-size-fits-all approach would not work.

Challenges and Strategies in Leadership

One significant challenge Yevgeni faced was during the acquisition of a company in Oslo. He started gently but had to increase pressure, resulting in some staff turnover. This experience highlighted the need for a delicate balance in managing transitions and maintaining team cohesion.

Yevgeni also realised that feeling like a foreigner from the beginning due to stigma and differences was something to actively embrace. Multilingualism played a crucial role in this, as it facilitated communication and understanding.

His background from the Balkans, a region characterised by small size and economic challenges, instilled in him the need to adjust and be flexible.

Cultural Adaptability and Empathy

Yevgeni's ability to adjust and remain humble rather than imposing his own will was key to his success as a manager.

He deployed snippets of empathy to create bonds and a sense of belonging among his team members.

This mental agility helped him avoid reverting to a comfort zone, an attitude that was not commonly discussed among his managerial peers who preferred to stay in their sense of comfort.

Most of Yevgeni's career was spent with Anglo-Saxon cultures, with one exception being a very French organisation with an Israeli founder.

He felt like a "fish out of water" in this setting,

considering French practices and work ethics as "alien."

Onboarding and Inclusivity

Yevgeni emphasised the importance of proper onboarding to ensure inclusivity. A recent example involved preparing a presentation for 20 Key Account Managers and managers from Spain and Germany, with the majority being French speakers.

Out of laziness or convenience, the French speakers pivoted to French without asking others for validation.

This habit made some managers feel excluded, and Yevgeni countered this by giving disproportionate attention to newcomers, allowing them time to speak and share their experiences as a source of enrichment.

Overcoming Isolation

Post-COVID, the shift to remote work created challenges in maintaining team cohesion and combating isolation. Yevgeni advocated at least one annual in-person meeting or team event, emphasising that nothing beats face-to-face interactions for building strong teams. He also promoted topical collaboration and cross-silo interactions to foster shared goals and collaboration.

Conclusion

Yevgeni's journey underscores the importance of cultural adaptability, empathy, and flexibility in leadership.

By embracing his multicultural background and continuously adjusting his management style to suit diverse teams, Yevgeni created an inclusive and cohesive work environment.

His experiences highlight the value of proper onboarding, in-person interactions, and continuous learning to navigate the complexities of leading multicultural teams effectively.

Understanding of a journey

Scores of selected countries during Yevgeni's interactions.

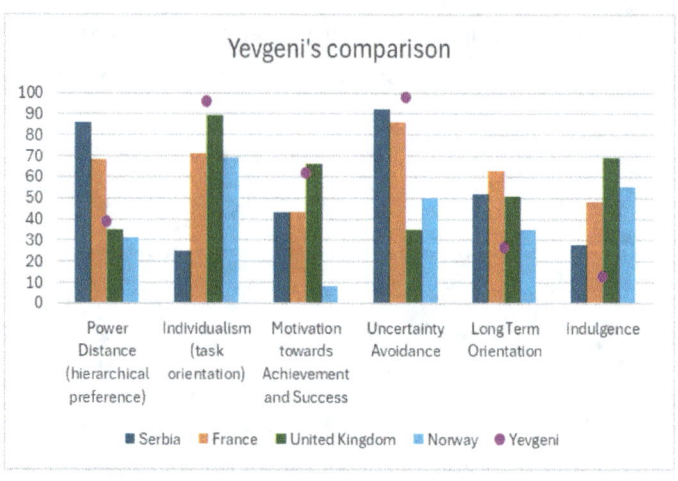

Reflection on Yevgeni's Culture Scores

Yevgeni's journey from a multicultural upbringing in Strasbourg to managing diverse teams across various countries highlights the complexity and adaptability required in leadership roles.

Power Distance Index (PDI)

Yevgeni's score of 39 in Power Distance suggests a preference for relatively equal power distribution and a dislike for hierarchical structures. This score is lower than the French score (68) and significantly lower than the Serbian score (86).

The gaps between Yevgeni's score and those of France and Serbia indicate that he may feel more comfortable in less hierarchical environments, where power is more evenly distributed. This preference aligns with his success in managing multicultural teams, where he likely encouraged a more egalitarian and inclusive management style.

The smaller gap with the UK score (35) suggests that Yevgeni felt more culturally aligned during his time in the UK, where similar attitudes toward power distribution are prevalent.

Individualism vs. Collectivism (IDV)

Yevgeni's score of 96 in Individualism reflects a strong emphasis on personal independence and self-expression, far exceeding the French (71) and Serbian (25) scores. This high level of Individualism likely influenced his leadership style, encouraging team members to take initiative and express their ideas freely. The gap with Serbia, in particular, might have presented challenges when dealing with more collectivist mindsets, where group harmony and consensus are prioritised over individual expression.

Assertiveness (MAS)

With a score of 62 in Assertiveness, Yevgeni values a balance between competitiveness and quality of life. This score shows that he places more importance on achievement and assertiveness than both the French (43) and Serbians (43).

The moderate gap suggests that while Yevgeni may have faced some cultural friction, he was able to navigate environments where a softer, more cooperative approach was expected, although as explained in the case with the team in Norway (8), this dimension was not always easy.

His ability to balance these values likely contributed to his success in managing teams across cultures with varying degrees of competitiveness.

Uncertainty Avoidance Index (UAI)

Yevgeni's score of 98 in Uncertainty Avoidance is exceptionally high, indicating a strong preference for structure, rules, and predictability. This score is slightly higher than the French (86) and Serbian (92) scores.

His high score suggests that he may prefer well-defined processes and clear expectations in the workplace, which could explain his careful approach to managing transitions and maintaining team cohesion.

The larger gap with the UK score (35) and Norway (50) implies that Yevgeni might have felt uncomfortable with the more relaxed and less structured approach prevalent in the UK and Norway.

Long-Term Orientation vs. Short-Term Normative Orientation (LTO)

Yevgeni's score of 27 in Long-Term Orientation indicates a preference for short-term goals, traditions, and quick results. This score is significantly lower than the French (63) and Serbian (52) scores, suggesting that Yevgeni is more focused on immediate outcomes rather than his French and Serbian co-workers.

The gap with France indicates that Yevgeni may have faced challenges in adapting to a culture that values perseverance and long-term thinking and felt more at home in a more fast-paced work environment, such as are common in the Anglo-Saxon world.

Indulgence vs. Restraint (IVR)

Yevgeni's score of 13 in Indulgence is very low, indicating a strong tendency toward restraint, self-discipline, and controlled gratification. This score is moderately lower than the French (48) and Serbian (28) scores.

The large gaps indicate that Yevgeni might have struggled with cultures that place a higher value on impulsiveness, enjoyment, and personal expression, such as the UK and Norway (69 and 55).

His preference for restraint likely influenced his leadership style, emphasising discipline and focus over spontaneity and indulgence.

Overall Reflection

Yevgeni's cultural scores reveal a complex interplay between his personal values and the cultural environments of France, the UK, Serbia, and Norway. His low Power Distance and high Individualism scores suggest that he values equality and personal autonomy, which may have set him apart in more hierarchical and collectivist cultures like France and Serbia.

His high Uncertainty Avoidance score indicates a preference for structure and predictability, which likely influenced his cautious approach to managing multicultural teams.

However, the significant gaps in Long-Term Orientation and Indulgence between Yevgeni and the cultures he interacted with might have led to challenges in adapting to environments that value long-term planning and a more relaxed approach to life.

Story 8 Via Veneto - Navigating Italy and Japan

Childhood and Local Distinctions

From a very young age, Stefano's life was marked by the experience of being a foreigner. When he was three years old, his parents divorced, and his mother returned to her childhood region, the Veneto region of Italy, a mid-sized town with a distinct culture.

Venice, where Stefano spent most of his early years, is a city with a proud and unique identity. Outside Venice, however, lay the farmlands, separated by a long bridge to Mestrino and beyond, areas often considered less sophisticated.

During the weekdays, Stefano went to school in Venice, but weekends were spent in the countryside. His friends in Venice would often ask him about "the farmland" with a mix of curiosity and good-natured teasing. Despite this teasing, he felt a deep connection to both places. Being from Veneto means embracing the region's independence, embodied by the political environment of the Lega Veneta and its strong symbols of autonomy. However, as he grew older, the pride he once felt began to wane as the politics of the region grew more contentious, and he found himself feeling like a foreigner even among those who valued being distinct from the rest of Italy.

Education and Early Adulthood

Stefano's academic journey took him to Ferrara and later to Milan. Ferrara, with its rich history and vibrant student life, was a stark contrast to the more rigid environment he was accustomed to in Venice. However, it was during his Erasmus exchange program in the Netherlands that he truly began to understand the diversity of European cultures. Living and studying alongside peers from all over Europe was a transformative experience. It broadened his perspectives and challenged his preconceived notions of identity and belonging.

Returning to Italy, he began his professional career in Milan, a city known for its acceptance and dynamic culture. Milan, much like New York City, embraces its diversity, allowing anyone to integrate and become part of the local fabric. This sense of belonging was a refreshing change from the more homogenous and insular communities he had previously known. In Milan, he felt welcomed and valued for his unique experiences and perspectives.

The Challenges of Homogeneity

However, Stefano's return to the Veneto region brought back the familiar feelings of being judged in and out of place. In homogenous societies like those in smaller Italian towns or even places like Tokyo, being different often means being an outsider.

The strong subcultures in cities like Milan and New York create an environment where diversity is celebrated, and everyone can find their place. In contrast, more homogenous places tend to be less accepting of those who do not fit the traditional mould.

His early work experience was in typical local branches of multinational companies, which at the time were not as diverse as they are today. The corporate culture was very male-dominated and hierarchical. This environment was challenging, especially during high-pressure situations like multinational pitches.

The lack of diversity and the rigid structure often left him feeling like he didn't belong as expressed in the following quote:

> *"Basically, you were constantly grinding, and every time you wanted to pitch in with ideas, you were shut down and expected to simply fall in line and do your job."*

Building a Diverse Agency

In 2006, Stefano decided to start his own agency, with a focus on social media, which was still a new and emerging field. He wanted to create something different, something inclusive. Inspired by the code of honour akin to the samurai, he aimed to build an organisation that valued diversity and empowered its employees. This vision attracted people who felt they didn't belong elsewhere, including members of the LGBTQ+ community.

His agency grew to 80 people, with more diversity than many multinationals at the time. They set a tone of inclusivity and gave real power to underrepresented groups, such as women, who then brought their own networks along. The reflection that everyone in the traditional corporate world looked the same made him realise the importance of diversity. It wasn't just about fitting in but about enriching the workplace with different perspectives and experiences.

Navigating Corporate Cultures

As an employee in more traditional settings, Stefano often felt out of place. The homogeneity was stifling, and he could imagine how much more challenging it must be for those who visibly differ from the norm. The language barrier also played a significant role. In Italy, if one didn't speak fluent Italian, they were often excluded from international projects, creating a full-on or full-off dynamic that was difficult to navigate.

Embracing Diversity and Inclusion

True belonging comes from valuing diversity. It's not about having an inclusion plan but about genuinely believing that differences enrich us. In a culture like Italy's, the leader must embody this belief and facilitate it. Stefano made it a point not to tolerate locker room talk or adolescent comments about women. Addressing these issues head-on created a "no jerks allowed" atmosphere, boosting the confidence of those being targeted and making the perpetrators feel awkward.

The Importance of Onboarding

Onboarding is often overlooked, but it's crucial for creating a welcoming environment. At their young agency, Stefano and his team wanted a structured onboarding process, but due to time constraints, it often felt more like a pool party. Everyone was welcomed the same way, but it lacked structure. Contrast this with experiences at larger firms, where even after three months, one might not feel integrated. This uncertainty and fatigue can make newcomers question their place.

A proper onboarding process should cover logistics, roles, and the overall way of working within the team. It should provide a clear code of conduct to help new employees start with trust and clarity, making change less traumatic.

The Japanese Experience

Stefano's journey took an unexpected turn when he first visited Japan 15 years ago. During that trip, he was stranded for a week due to an Icelandic volcano eruption. This unplanned stay sparked his interest in Japanese culture, particularly Sake. He eventually became a Sake ambassador for Japan in Italy. This connection to Japan deepened when he met his future wife, a Japanese woman. Her father's questions, like whether he had a bathtub at home, highlighted the cultural differences they would navigate together.

Now, they run a small travel agency organizing trips to Japan, where they try to share the cultural richness of the country with others. Stefano's son, being half-Japanese, experiences the duality of being considered "half" in Japan and "double" in Italy, a testament to the complex nature of multicultural identity. As Stefano stated during our interview:

> *"The core of embracing diversity lies in how differences in opinion are handled. When someone says, 'I do not agree with you,' it sets the foundation for either shutting down or exploring new perspectives. This openness to diverse opinions enriches us and helps create a more inclusive environment."*

Reflection and Moving Forward

Reflecting on his journey, Stefano has come to understand that being a foreigner is a complex and multifaceted experience. It's not just about geographical location but about navigating cultural, social, and professional landscapes. Embracing diversity, fostering inclusivity, and valuing different perspectives have been key to his personal and professional growth.

As he continues to navigate the cultural spectrum, Stefano strives to create environments where everyone can feel a sense of belonging, where diversity is not just accepted but celebrated. This journey has taught him that being a foreigner can be a source of strength, resilience, and profound understanding, enriching both his life and the lives of those around him.

Understanding of a journey

Scores of selected countries based on Stefano's journey:

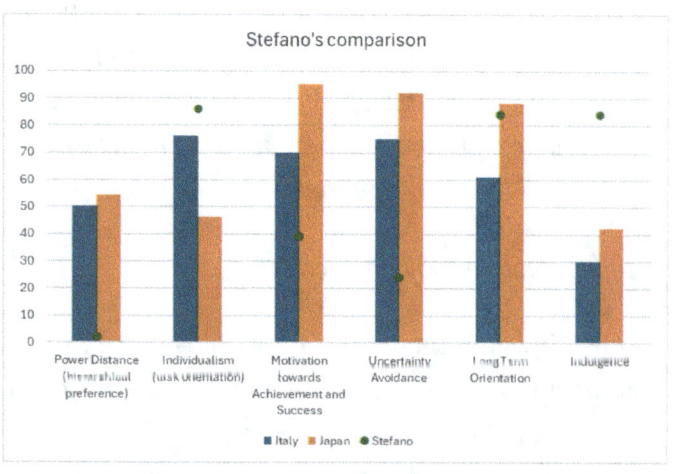

Reflection on Stefano's Culture Scores

Stefano's journey, marked by experiences in Italy and Japan, provides a compelling backdrop for understanding how his cultural values have shaped his interactions and personal growth. By examining Stefano's Culture Compass scores and comparing them to the values of Italy and Japan, we can gain a deeper insight into the cultural dynamics that have influenced his life and professional experiences.

Power Distance Index (PDI)

Stefano's score of 2 in Power Distance is exceptionally low, indicating a strong preference for equality and minimal hierarchical structures. This score is much lower than both the Italian (50) and Japanese scores (54). The significant gap between Stefano's score and those of Italy and Japan likely influenced his decision to create a diverse and inclusive agency, where power dynamics are minimised, and everyone's voice is valued. Stefano's discomfort with hierarchical structures may have also contributed to his feeling of being out of place in more traditional and hierarchical corporate settings.

Individualism vs. Collectivism (IDV)

With a score of 86 in Individualism, Stefano highly values personal independence and self-expression. This score is significantly higher than Japan (46) and somewhat higher than Italy (76), more likely so outside the bigger cities, where Italy tends to score even more collectivistic.

His high Individualism score aligns with his experience in Milan, a city known for its dynamic and accepting culture, which allowed him to thrive by embracing his unique perspectives.

However, this strong individualism may have made it

challenging for Stefano to adapt to the more collectivist norms in Japan, where group harmony often takes precedence over individual expression.

Assertiveness (MAS)

Stefano's score of 39 in assertiveness reflects a moderate emphasis on cooperation, quality of life, and nurturing roles over competitiveness and assertiveness. This score suggests that Stefano values a more balanced approach between achievement and quality of life than the Italians (70) and Japanese (95).

The substantial gaps likely motivated him to build an organisation that values diversity and inclusivity, where collaboration and mutual respect are prioritised over aggressive competition.

Uncertainty Avoidance Index (UAI)

Stefano's score of 24 in Uncertainty Avoidance is quite low, indicating a strong comfort with ambiguity and a preference for flexibility and spontaneity. This score is significantly lower than both the Italian (75) and Japanese (92) scores.

This low score likely enabled him to navigate the uncertainties of starting his own agency and embracing new and emerging fields like social media.

However, the large gaps with Italy and Japan suggest that Stefano may have struggled with the more rigid and risk-averse aspects of these cultures, potentially feeling stifled by the emphasis on rules and predictability.

Long-Term Orientation vs. Short-Term Normative Orientation (LTO)

Stefano's score of 84 in Long-Term Orientation reflects a strong focus on future planning, perseverance, and long-term goals. This score is significantly higher than Italy (61) and would be even more so with the current Italian cultural score of 39. His preference is very close to the Japanese score of 88 (and nowadays 100).

The gaps likely influenced his strategic decisions, such as his dedication to building a sustainable and inclusive business. The smaller gap with Japan indicates that Stefano's long-term planning aligns more closely with Japanese cultural values, which may have helped him navigate and appreciate aspects of Japanese culture, particularly in his professional dealings and personal life.

Indulgence vs. Restraint (IVR)

Stefano's score of 84 in Indulgence indicates a strong inclination towards enjoying life and embracing personal freedom. This score is much higher than both the Italian (30) and Japanese (42) scores, indicating that Stefano may have found the more restrained and disciplined cultures of Italy and Japan to be somewhat at odds with his own desire for enjoyment and personal freedom.

This emphasis on indulgence likely influenced his approach to creating a work environment that fosters well-being and encourages employees to bring their whole selves to work.

Overall Reflection

Stefano's cultural scores reveal a complex interplay between his personal values and the cultural environments of Italy and Japan.

His low Power Distance and Uncertainty Avoidance scores suggest that he values egalitarianism and flexibility, which may have set him apart in more hierarchical and risk-averse settings in Italy and Japan.

His high Individualism and Indulgence scores indicate a strong preference for personal freedom and self-expression, which may have driven his success in more dynamic and diverse environments like Milan.

However, the significant gaps in Power Distance,

Uncertainty Avoidance, and Indulgence between Stefano and the cultures he interacted with might have led to periods of adjustment and cultural tension, especially in more traditional and homogenous settings.

Story 9 Navigating Identity and Leadership – A Journey from Cork to Corporate America

In the following chapter, we follow the westward journey of Nick, an Irishman in his late fifties, who grew up in Cork Harbour, with a Marine Engineer father, a mother who was a nurse and two younger sisters. Nick's journey brings us a unique engineering perspective into people management and takes us into the perspective of realising how religious background and age impacted behaviour.

Early Years in Cork

Growing up in a semi-urbanized village in Cork,

Ireland, next to the river, was a unique experience for Nick.

The presence of boats was a constant, and they became a significant part of his life. His father, a college lecturer, provided a middle-class upbringing, though it wasn't something they discussed much. The juxtaposition of their home against a tougher, more dangerous housing estate behind them shaped Nick's early perceptions.

As Nick mentioned from this memory:

> *"While they - the kids from the middle-class area - had real boats, the kids from the estate excelled in building rafts,"*

displaying a skill that he admired in terms of figuring things out on the go and making things work with what you had at hand.

Nick's education began at a convent school, where nuns imparted a strict and conservative education. At the age of seven, he transitioned to a mixed state school, a shift that initially saw his academic performance dip before he found his footing again.

Secondary school took him to a monastery, returning to the all-male education trend. With a lineage of engineers in the family—his father and grandfather both being engineers—it was almost predestined that he would follow a similar path.

Entering the Workforce

Graduating from Cork Institute of Technology, Nick embarked on his professional journey with a small company conducting cable testing and surveys across the country. This entry-level job was followed by a role at an American computer components manufacturer, where he engaged in manufacturing testing quality.

The monotony of the work led him to a new position supervising a manufacturing line, where he discovered the challenges of working with people. It was here that he started learning about Just in Time manufacturing (Lean), participating in an EU program on lean manufacturing at Galway Campus, and later pursuing an MBA at University College Galway.

The technical focus was a real challenge but building business cases with higher ROI intrigued Nick more. This new interest led to being headhunted by a USA company looking for someone with a unique combination of engineering, mountaineering, and an MBA.

He ran the business in Cork for 10 years, during which Declan, a consultant, significantly influenced his career trajectory by challenging him to aspire to much greater potential. Eventually, Nick became the president of the US operations, and in the process, he moved his family to the USA with a focus on state school location to ensure continuity in the upbringing of his children.

Clashes and Transitions

Running the USA company for a decade was a period of immense learning and growth for Nick. However, a strategic clash with the founder led him to work for a private equity group to turn around a tooling (knife) company. This stint lasted four years, ending when the business was sold during COVID. Post-pandemic, he started an independent group and joined an industrial controls technology company, running two plants in Washington and Oregon, which were eventually purchased by another business.

Cultural Encounters and Adaptations

Nick's first encounters with people of Protestant background revealed differences in behaviour and social norms. The older generation was aloof, while the younger ones seemed lost, yet typically better behaved and very polite.

This cultural observation extended to his professional life, distinguishing between the engineering class and the operating class. Despite initially feeling he knew more, he quickly realised his ignorance. The housing estate experience had instilled in him a sense of equality and respect, devoid of ego, which proved invaluable in union interactions.

He realised early on that most differences are superficial. Once you get to know people, there are zero differences—the veneer is merely cultural norms imprinted upon them. Nick encountered little prejudice, but sometimes, people erected walls to protect their identities. Instead of breaking down these walls, he learned to navigate alongside them, asking questions rather than providing answers, fostering camaraderie.

Professional Evolution and Leadership

Throughout his career, time management and prioritisation were crucial for Nick. Shifting from field sports to martial arts, and eventually bouldering, he adopted a mental aikido approach, solving problems by finding the key.

Management by walking around provided a significant return on investment, as it allowed him to collect clues and understand the nuances of the workplace.

Onboarding experiences varied. As a graduate

engineer, he was put on a harness assembly line, supervising operations while building them. At the American computer component manufacturer, he was immersed in a team with a shared experience, fostering connections.

Joining the 2nd US corporation, he was brought to the USA for three months, a clear and focused onboarding process. During his stint at the tooling company, as the new CEO, he interviewed everyone, which disrupted the previous top-down dynamic, fostering a sense of belonging.

Building and Maintaining Relationships

Creating a symbiotic relationship between formal onboarding and breaking down perceived levels was essential for Nick. Terminating relationships with respect, even with so-called enemies, was a crucial lesson. Maintaining relationships post-termination, as exemplified by a Swiss distributor who earned more during the earn-out stage than when distributing, was a testament to this approach.

Reflecting on his journey, Nick realised that building a sense of community, valuing team spirit, and fostering inclusivity were vital. Whether it was navigating cultural differences, managing teams, or leading companies, the underlying principle remained the same—understanding, respect, and collaboration are the keys to successful leadership and personal fulfilment.

Understanding of a journey

Scores of selected countries in Nick's story.

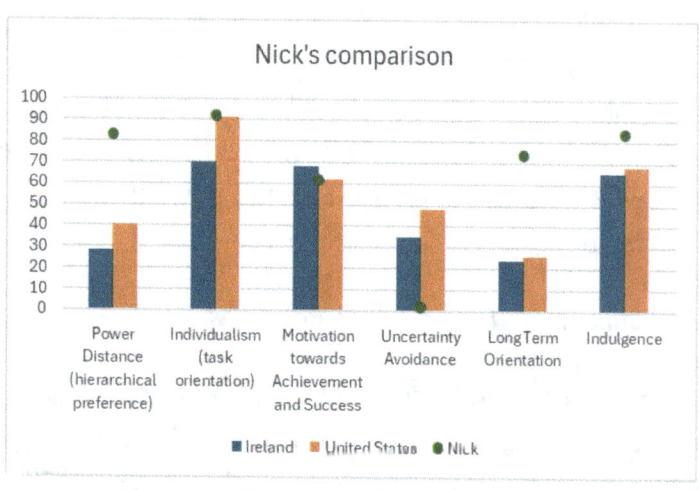

Reflection on Nick's Culture Scores

Nick's journey from Cork, Ireland, to corporate America offers a rich context for understanding how his cultural values shaped his experiences and leadership style.

By examining Nick's Culture Compass scores and comparing them to the values of Ireland and the United States, we can gain a deeper insight into how these cultural dynamics influenced his life and career.

Power Distance Index (PDI)

Nick's score of 83 in Power Distance is significantly higher than both the Irish (28) and U.S. scores (40). The large gap between Nick's score and the Irish scores indicates that he may have felt out of sync with the more egalitarian and less hierarchical norms in Ireland.

This difference might have influenced his initial discomfort or adjustment challenges in his early career in Ireland. Despite the large gap with the U.S. score, Nick may have found the hierarchical nature of corporate America more aligned with his personal preferences, which could explain his success in rising to leadership positions there.

Individualism vs. Collectivism (IDV)

With a score of 92 in Individualism, Nick strongly values personal independence and self-expression. This score is higher than the Irish (70) and close to the original score in the United States (91), which mostly resembles white America.

Today's score of 60 for the United States is more representative for the whole country. The gap indicates that Nick may have felt more individualistic than his peers in Ireland, possibly leading to a sense of being different or out of place in a culture that traditionally valued community and collective well-being. However, his high Individualism score aligns closely with the United States, where individual achievement and autonomy are highly valued.

This alignment most likely facilitated Nick's transition to the USA, where he could thrive in a culture that matched his personal values.

Assertiveness (MAS)

Nick's score of 62 in Assertiveness reflects a moderate emphasis on competitiveness and achievement. This score is close to both the Irish (68) and USA (62) scores. The small gap suggests that Nick did not experience significant cultural dissonance in terms of gender roles or competitiveness in either Ireland or the USA.

Uncertainty Avoidance Index (UAI)

Nick's score of 2 in Uncertainty Avoidance is extremely low, indicating strong comfort with ambiguity and a preference for flexibility and spontaneity. This score is drastically lower than the Irish (35) and U.S. (48) scores.

This low score likely enabled him to embrace challenges and changes throughout his career, whether in Ireland or in the United States. However, it may have also caused friction when working with others who preferred more structure and predictability, potentially leading to misunderstandings or differing approaches to problem-solving.

Long-Term Orientation vs. Short-Term Normative Orientation (LTO)

Nick's score of 74 in Long-Term Orientation reflects a strong focus on future planning, perseverance, and long-term goals. This score is higher than both the Irish (24) and American (26) scores. The gap suggests that Nick may prioritise long-term success and adaptability more than his peers, which could have driven his career decisions, such as pursuing an MBA and moving to the USA for better opportunities. This future-oriented mindset likely contributed to his ability to navigate complex corporate environments and achieve sustained success.

Indulgence vs. Restraint (IVR)

Nick's score of 84 in Indulgence indicates a strong inclination towards enjoying life and embracing personal freedom. This score is higher than both the Irish (65) and U.S. (68) scores.

This high Indulgence score may have influenced his work-life balance and approach to leadership, emphasising the importance of creating a work environment where people can thrive personally as well as professionally. The relatively small gap with the USA score suggests that he likely found a cultural fit in America that allowed him to maintain this balance.

Overall Reflection

Nick's cultural scores reveal a complex interplay between his personal values and the cultural environments of Ireland and the United States. His high Power Distance and Individualism scores suggest that he values hierarchy and personal autonomy, which may have set him apart in Ireland but found resonance in the USA.

His low Uncertainty Avoidance indicates a comfort with ambiguity that likely enabled him to adapt and thrive in various challenging situations, both in Ireland and the USA.

However, the significant gaps in Power Distance and Uncertainty Avoidance between Nick and the cultures he interacted with might have led to periods of adjustment and cultural tension, especially early in his career.

Story 10: Embracing Change – A Journey from Finland to the World

Sometimes it is those who are most similar to us which surprise us the most. In this story, we look at Finland before it opened up to the world. Finland was a place where even speaking with a slightly different accent could expose you as a "foreigner," as witnessed in this journey by Erika, a Finnish woman in her fifties, who grew up in Leppävirta, in central Finland with her parents and a brother four years younger.

A Small Village in Finland

Growing up in a very small village in Finland, Erika lived in a world that felt isolated and homogeneous. Foreigners were a rarity, and her only exposure to different perspectives came through learning English. Eager to connect with the wider world, she joined a pen pal association.

This decision brought her pen pals from Canada and Northern Ireland, opening her eyes to new cultures and ideas. At just 12 years old, Erika resolved that her first step after high school would be to travel to the USA.

Dreams Realised in the USA

True to her word, Erika moved to the USA as an au pair right after high school. This experience felt like a dream come true. Growing up, her village had been the central hub for surrounding smaller villages, each with its own distinct identity despite being only 10 kilometres apart.

In school, clear in-groups and out-groups formed, particularly with a tight-knit group from Sorsakoski, a steel industry village in Savo, Eastern Finland. Erika's time as an au pair in Washington DC and New York City was a stark contrast to her small village life. The melting pot of cultures and the openness of the people were everything she had dreamed of since she was 12, as Erika described it:

> *"Everyone was smiling, welcoming, and diverse, it just felt so much more positive."*

The Challenge of Returning Home

Returning to Finland after such an enriching experience in the USA was challenging. The transition back to her village was difficult, and Erika felt out of place. Her family's roots were in Lapland, so she decided to live there for a while, hoping to find a sense of belonging.

Lapland, specifically Kilpisjärvi, was a different world altogether. Here, she encountered the Poromiehet - reindeer herders - and many foreign tourists, including those from the Utti airbase. She often hitchhiked to Norway, exploring new horizons.

However, Erika still didn't feel at home whenever she visited her home region of Savo. With a mother from Oulu and a father from Lapland, she had no strong ties to any one place. Even the dialect they spoke at home was different from that in Savo, further alienating her.

In the USA, Erika had felt an immediate sense of belonging. The language was inclusive, and the possibilities seemed endless. In Lapland, the straightforward way of talking felt more familiar, in contrast to the gossiping nature of Savo. The directness of the Lapland dialect resonated with her, much like the straightforwardness she appreciated in the USA.

Academic and Professional Journey

Erika excelled in school, but choosing a field of study was difficult. Eventually, she pursued an MA in economics, focusing on the tourism and travel industry. During her studies, she worked in sales, marketing, and customer service for five years. After graduation, she continued in this industry before transitioning to the academic side as a study affairs officer. This role took her from Vaasa to Helsinki, where she continued to work in travel and tourism.

Her ex-husband's career in academia led Erika to a University of Applied Sciences degree in business management. This position offered her the opportunity to see the world again through the lens of education and international exchange.

Building Community in the Tourism Industry

Erika's first job in the tourism industry was built around a strong sense of community, a hallmark of the field. One initial barrier was language, as many colleagues spoke Swedish as their mother tongue. Her own Swedish skills were limited to "pakko-ruotsi" (the mandatory Swedish taught in Finnish schools), but she took the initiative to learn. Colleagues supported her in this endeavour, and her efforts to integrate into the new environment paid off.

Creating a Welcoming Environment

In her current role, Erika focuses on making new people feel at home. As the person responsible for exchange students, she provides mental support and strives to be approachable without relying on any stereotypes. Erika believes in offering robust support systems, such as a buddy system and integration into new study projects. This approach helps new students navigate their new environment and feel welcomed and valued.

Reflection and Forward

Reflecting on her journey from a small village in Finland to various parts of the world, Erika is grateful for the diverse experiences that have shaped her perspective. Each phase of her life has taught her the importance of community, inclusivity, and the willingness to embrace new cultures. Her journey underscores the value of taking initiative and supporting others in their transition to new environments.

As Erika continues to work in academia and support exchange students, she carries these lessons with her. She strives to create spaces where everyone can feel a sense of belonging and be empowered to succeed. The journey from Finland to the world and back again has been one of growth, learning, and the continuous pursuit of connection and understanding.

Understanding of a journey

Scores of selected countries from Erika's story.

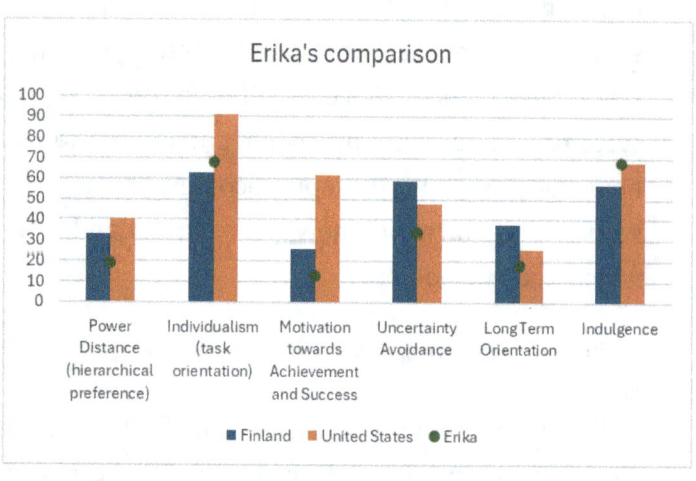

Reflection on Erika's Culture Scores

Erika's journey from a small village in Finland to various parts of the world, and back again, provides a fascinating context for understanding her cultural scores. By examining Erika's Culture Compass scores and comparing them to Finnish and American cultural values, we can gain deeper insights into her experiences and the cultural challenges she navigated.

Power Distance (PDI)

Erika's score of 19 in Power Distance is notably low, reflecting a strong preference for egalitarian relationships and minimal hierarchical structures. This aligns well with Finnish culture, which also has a low Power Distance score of 33, resulting in a small gap of 14 points.

This suggests that Erika is comfortable in environments where authority is decentralised, and equality is emphasised.

However, when compared to the United States, where Power Distance is slightly higher at 40, Erika's preference for flat structures might have clashed somewhat with the more hierarchical elements she encountered, especially in academic settings.

This difference, though not extreme, could have influenced her sense of belonging and her ability to navigate authority-driven environments.

Individualism (IDV)

Erika's score of 68 in Individualism indicates a strong orientation towards individual achievement and personal freedom, which is only slightly above the Finnish score of 63. This small difference suggests that Erika's values are generally closely aligned with the Finnish emphasis on personal autonomy. However, when compared to the United States, which has a higher Individualism score of 91, Erika might have felt more at home in American culture, particularly in the diverse and individualistic environment she experienced as an au pair.

This alignment likely contributed to her sense of belonging during her time in the USA, where individual expression and independence are highly valued and offered her a new window for self-realisation.

Assertiveness (MAS)

With a score of 13 in assertiveness, Erika displays a strong preference for modesty, care for others, and quality of life over competitiveness and achievement. This score is moderately lower than both the Finnish score of 26 and the American score of 62.

This difference could explain why Erika found the directness and community-focused aspects of Lapland appealing, as they resonated with her low assertiveness score.

Conversely, in environments that were more

competitive or achievement-driven, such as certain academic or corporate settings, Erika may have felt out of place or at odds with the prevailing cultural norms.

Uncertainty Avoidance (UAI)

Erika's score of 34 in Uncertainty Avoidance suggests a relatively low level of anxiety about uncertainty and a greater openness to new experiences. This is lower than the Finnish score of 59. This trait likely served her well during her travels and in adapting to different cultural environments, such as the United States.

Her ability to embrace uncertainty and adapt to new situations would have been crucial in navigating the various challenges she faced, particularly in her return to Finland and her work in the tourism and academic sectors.

Long-Term Orientation (LTO)

Erika's score of 18 in Long-Term Orientation reflects a strong preference for short-term goals and traditions over long-term planning and perseverance. This score is significantly lower than Finland's score of 35. This gap could have contributed to her challenges in readjusting to Finnish society after her time abroad, as her experiences in the USA (scoring 26 at the time) might have reinforced a more immediate and dynamic approach to life, contrasting with Finland's more future- focused mindset expressed in Finland's cultural score today (63).

The gap is also pronounced when compared to the United States' score of 50 today, suggesting that while she may have found American culture to be more in tune with her short-term orientation at the time of her visit, doing it again today might be a different experience altogether.

Indulgence (IVR)

Erika's score of 68 in Indulgence indicates a high value on enjoying life and the importance of leisure time, which is slightly higher than the Finnish score of 57. This attitude aligns well with the cultural values of the United States, which shares the same Indulgence score of 68.

This alignment likely contributed to Erika's positive experiences in the USA, where the culture supports a more indulgent lifestyle. However, this orientation might have made it difficult for her to readjust to the more restrained Finnish environment upon her return.

Overall Reflection

When reflecting on Erika's cultural scores and comparing them to the Finnish and American cultural values, it becomes clear that her personal values are somewhat aligned with both, yet distinct in key areas.

Erika's low Power Distance, strong Individualism, and high Indulgence scores suggest that she values equality, personal freedom, and the enjoyment of life—traits that served her well during her time in the USA and in her efforts to create welcoming environments for others in her professional life.

However, the significant gaps in Long-Term Orientation and relative gap in assertiveness indicate that Erika may have felt out of sync with certain aspects of Finnish culture, particularly its emphasis on future planning and competitiveness.

These differences likely contributed to her feelings of alienation upon returning to Finland, as well as the challenges she faced in finding her place within more hierarchical or achievement-driven environments.

Part 3: Strategies

Ten Key Takeaways on Adapting When You Feel Out of Place

The stories in this book illustrate the diverse experiences of individuals who have navigated feelings of foreignerness in various cultural contexts. Through their journeys, they have shared valuable insights on how to adapt when you feel out of place. Here are the ten main takeaways:

1. Embrace Emotional Intelligence and Self-Reflection

Kalle's story as the CEO of Teravamuoti highlights the importance of developing emotional intelligence and practising self-reflection. Recognising how his behaviour affected others allowed him to navigate conflicts and build a more inclusive team. By understanding your own emotional triggers and learning to manage them, you can better adapt to new cultural environments and lead effectively.

2. Adapt Communication Styles to Bridge Cultural Gaps

John's experience as an aviation trainer across different continents demonstrates the necessity of adapting communication styles.

Whether dealing with language barriers or differing cultural expectations, keeping communication as short and simple as possible is key. Simplifying your language, being mindful of cultural nuances, and ensuring that your message is understood can help build trust and avoid misunderstandings.

3. Leverage Multilingualism for Inclusivity

Yevgeni's journey through diverse cultural settings underscores the value of multilingualism in fostering inclusivity.

Learning new languages and immersing yourself in different cultures can help bridge gaps and build rapport.

By making an effort to communicate in the local language or understanding regional dialects, you show respect and openness to the host culture, which can ease the feeling of being an outsider.

4. Find Common Ground Through Shared Experiences

Jan's story of moving from the Netherlands to the USA, Belgium, and Finland highlights the importance of finding common ground. By engaging in shared activities, such as mentoring programs or community events, you can create a sense of belonging and mutual understanding. These shared experiences help overcome cultural barriers and foster connections with those who might initially seem different.

5. Balance Cultural Sensitivity with Authenticity

Stefano's experience in Italy and Japan teaches us to balance cultural sensitivity with authenticity. While it is essential to respect local customs and adapt to cultural norms, staying true to your values and identity is equally important. Finding this balance allows you to build genuine relationships and gain respect from others, even in unfamiliar settings.

6. Foster Open and Inclusive Environments in moderation

Anni's global career journey illustrates the importance of creating environments that are open and inclusive. By encouraging open dialogue, active participation, and mutual respect, you can help others feel comfortable and valued. This approach is particularly crucial when working with multicultural teams, as it promotes understanding and reduces the feeling of foreignerness among team members.

However, not all cultural contexts are naturally supportive of people who are (very) different. So in those environments, go slow, enable people to get used to different ways one step at a time.

7. Practise Continuous Learning and Flexibility

Adrian's transition from the US to Europe shows the significance of continuous learning and flexibility. Embracing new experiences, whether through formal education or informal cultural exchanges, helps you stay adaptable in diverse environments. Being open to learning from others and adjusting your approach as needed will enable you to thrive in different cultural contexts.

8. Understand and Respect Hierarchies

John's leadership experiences across hierarchical and egalitarian cultures highlight the need to understand and respect local power dynamics. Recognising the level of hierarchy in a given culture and adjusting your leadership style accordingly can help you build rapport and influence effectively. Being aware of these dynamics enables you to navigate complex social and organisational structures more smoothly.

9. Build Empathy Through Exposure and Practice

Yevgeni's success in managing multicultural teams emphasises the role of empathy in leadership. By actively seeking to understand others' perspectives and adapting your management style to accommodate diverse needs, you can create a more harmonious and effective team environment.

Empathy is cultivated through exposure to different cultures and the practice of humility and listening.

10. Leverage Your Unique Background as a Strength

Throughout these stories, a common thread is the idea of leveraging your unique background as a source of strength. Whether it's Kalle's Finnish roots, John's experience as a South African pilot, or Jan's multicultural upbringing, each protagonist has used their distinct background to offer a fresh perspective and solve problems creatively.

Embracing your uniqueness allows you to contribute valuable insights and find your niche in any environment.

Recommendations for Organisations: Learning from the 10 Lessons on Adapting to Cultural Differences

Based on the ten key takeaways from the diverse stories in this book, here are three strategic recommendations for organisations aiming to create inclusive, culturally adaptable environments:

1. Promote Continuous Cultural Learning and Development

Outcome: A workforce that is not only aware of but also comfortable with cultural differences, leading to improved collaboration, reduced misunderstandings, and a more inclusive workplace.

Organisations should invest in ongoing cultural competence training and development programs. These programs involve more than just a one-time workshop; it means creating a continuous learning environment where employees are encouraged to engage with different cultures actively.

- Implementation Steps:
    - Develop training modules focused on emotional intelligence, communication styles, and cross-cultural understanding, using real-world scenarios similar to those faced

by individuals like Kalle, John, and Anni.
  - Facilitate language learning opportunities and cultural exchange programs to foster empathy and understanding, as seen in Yevgeni's and Jan's stories.
  - Encourage employees to participate in immersive experiences, such as international assignments, mentoring across cultures, or community engagement activities that reflect diverse cultural norms.

2. Create Inclusive Policies and Practices that Balance Adaptation with Authenticity

Outcome: An organisational culture that fosters a sense of belonging and authenticity, helping employees feel valued for their unique contributions and reducing turnover.

Organisations should strive to balance the need for employees to adapt to organisational culture while also respecting and valuing their unique cultural backgrounds. This step involves developing policies and practices that promote inclusivity without forcing assimilation.

- Implementation Steps:

- Introduce flexible policies that accommodate diverse cultural practices, such as flexible holidays for cultural or religious observances, dress codes that respect cultural norms, and inclusive language use in communications.
- Encourage employee resource groups (ERGs) or affinity groups that allow employees to share their cultural experiences and provide feedback on inclusivity efforts.
- Implement leadership development programs that train managers to balance cultural sensitivity with authenticity, as shown in Stefano's and Adrian's experiences, where they remained true to their values while adapting to different cultural settings.

3. Leverage Cultural Diversity as a Strategic Asset

Outcome: A more innovative, competitive organisation that leverages cultural diversity to its advantage, driving growth and performance in an increasingly globalised market.

Organisations should view cultural diversity not just

as a challenge but as a strategic asset that can drive innovation, creativity, and global competitiveness. This attitude requires intentionally harnessing the diverse perspectives and experiences of employees to solve complex problems and explore new opportunities.

- **Implementation Steps:**
  - Establish cross-functional and multicultural teams to encourage diverse perspectives in decision-making and problem-solving, mirroring the adaptability and flexibility shown by Yevgeni in managing multicultural teams.
  - Recognise and reward employees who demonstrate cultural competence and adaptability, promoting these skills as valuable assets for career advancement.
  - Create platforms for employees to share their experiences and insights from different cultural contexts, much like the diverse experiences of Jan, Yevgeni, and John, to foster innovation and new approaches to work.

Conclusion: Moving Towards a Culturally Inclusive Future

By promoting continuous learning, creating inclusive policies, and leveraging diversity as a strategic asset, organisations can learn from the lessons of adaptability and cultural navigation highlighted in this book. These strategies will help create a workplace environment where every employee, regardless of their background, feels included, valued, and empowered to contribute to the organisation's success.

As mentioned earlier in the book, as an organisation, we at The Culture Factor continue to update national cultural value scores every decade. Cultures do not change over a year, so we sometimes might underestimate the speed at which cultures change when they change.

Either way, whichever culture we find ourselves in, the likelihood of dealing with a diverse team has increased. As such, this chapter summarises our book with a reflection of "what if" these ten interviewees would come together, and you'd need to be managing them?

In exploring this "what if," I will take on the role of manager, with my personal cultural value preferences shown.

When we coach managers of international teams, one of our tools is creating a so-called "Landscape analysis"; in other words, visualising where we can spot certain trends.

Using our interviewees' and manager's score, this team development scenario would look like the following, including the observations derived from the analysis.

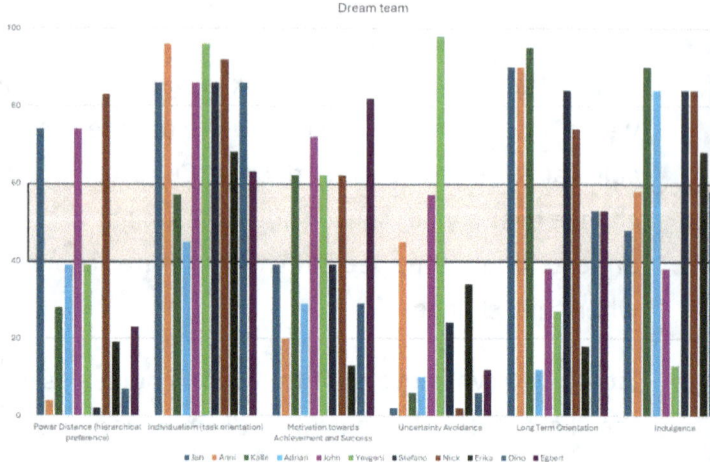

Using the landscape analysis as basis, we can create a "heat map".

The heat map showcases where the emotional differences between manager and direct reports and among direct reports are large (warm) or small (cold) – meaning that potentially "explosive" issues can be flagged before they happen, helping to keep the temperature in a room comfortable for all involved.

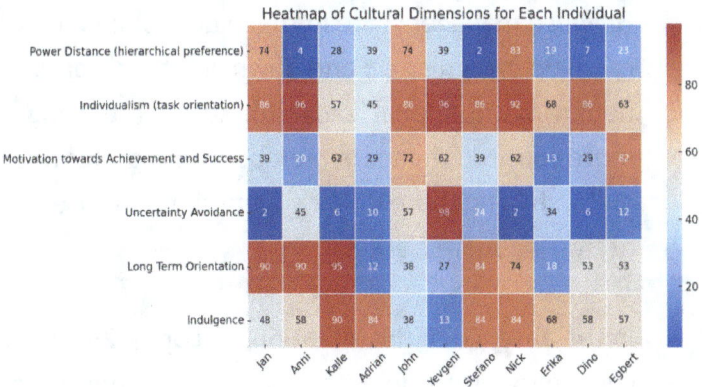

The lighter blue or red the colour, the lesser the difference between the manager and their team members.

The stronger the colour difference the more attention will be needed.

The bandwidth between scores 40-60 indicates a focus area where you, as a manager, can find cultural navigators or bridge builders - people who will find it emotionally easier to pivot between extremes.

1. Power Distance (Hierarchical Preference)

- There's a clear divide in the group between those who prefer hierarchical structures, such as Nick (83) and Jan (74), and those who lean toward egalitarian setups, like Stefano (2), Dino (7), and Anni (4).
- Most individuals fall on the extremes of this dimension, with few in the middle range.

Having a manager score in the middle band (40-60) can help in leading up and down, in other words, deploying situational leadership styles, providing more space to the team members who prefer less hierarchy and more direct supervision to those preferring more clarity.

In the absence of this situation, I (scoring 23) could choose to form a delegated style with either Adrian or Yevgeni in order to ensure clarity is provided to those who need it most (Nick and Jan).

2. Individualism (Task Orientation)

- The majority of the group shows a strong preference for individualism, with several members, including Anni, Yevgeni, John, and Nick, scoring above 85.
- A few individuals, such as Kalle (57), Adrian (45), and Erika (68), exhibit a more balanced approach, leaning toward group orientation without completely rejecting individualism.

Having a manager score in the middle band (40-60) can help in striking a balance between task execution and creating strong relationship bonds.

My score of 63 indicates that I can provide balance to ensure that the otherwise rather task-oriented focus of most team members does not lead to the exclusion of those with preferences aimed at relationships, such as Adrian and Kalle.

In the case of adding any individual into this team who prefers a stronger sense of collectivism, Adrian could be leveraged as their buddy while onboarding them, given his score.

3. Motivation Towards Achievement and Success

- The group is mixed in terms of achievement motivation. While some individuals like John (72), Kalle (62), and Yevgeni (62) are highly driven by success, others like Erika (13) and Anni (20) show much lower motivation levels.
- This dimension shows significant variability, with some members clearly prioritising personal success more than others.

My largest challenge as a manager will be to moderate my assertiveness and success orientation (82) given that most team members score significantly lower.

This can impact preferences for among others meeting styles. I could use Jan and Stefano as sounding boards with regards to when I push too much and or take decisions too fast, to ensure that the team members who prefer a more consensus-based approach feel more included in the decision-making.

In most multicultural teams we at The Culture Factor Group assess, there tends to be a strong split over this dimension, often impacting an important part of feelings of belonging and inclusion.

A practice we therefore recommend is what we call the DDEE cycle (Discuss, Decide, Execute, Evaluate).

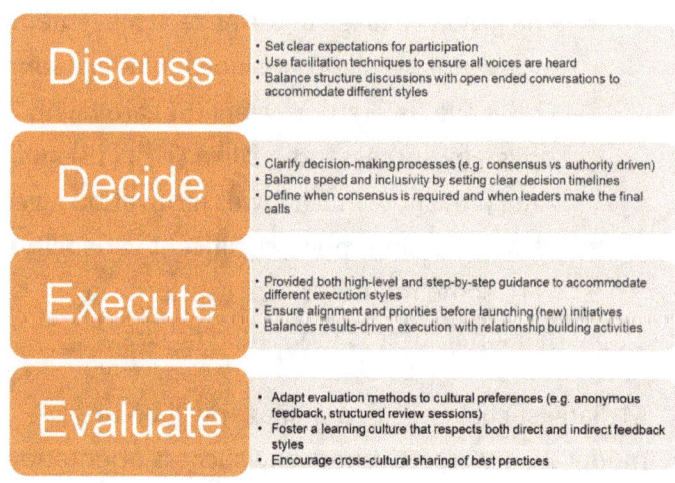

Be clear on when is the time for discussing, when is the time (and what are the grounds for) for deciding, then executing and only upon completion of the execution bit open up the floor for evaluating - this helps to ensure enough speed for those wishing to execute, and enough space for participation for those who prioritise consensus.

4. Uncertainty Avoidance

- There's a broad spectrum in comfort with uncertainty. On one end, Yevgeni (98) strongly avoids ambiguity, while individuals like Jan (2), Nick (2), Stefano (24), and Dino (6) show a much higher tolerance for uncertainty.
- This is one of the more polarised dimensions, with only a few individuals in the middle range, showing a balance between comfort and discomfort with uncertainty.

Overall, this team scores rather low on Uncertainty Avoidance, but with one strong outlier. In order to ensure Yevgeni could be kept onboard, I (12) would need to ensure good relationships with Anni and Nick in order to ensure enough predictability is provided for Yevgeni to feel comfortable enough, which would be especially important if this team were tasked to, for example, creating more structure in an organization, where a higher score for uncertainty avoidance can be an important asset.

5. Long Term Orientation

- Several individuals, such as Kalle (95), Jan (90), and Anni (90), are highly long-term focused, planning for the future and showing a strategic outlook.

- On the other end, members like Adrian (12), Erika (18), and Yevgeni (27) lean more toward short-term thinking, emphasising immediate goals and outcomes over future planning.

Similar to Uncertainty Avoidance, the team scores more towards one direction, in this case Long Term Orientation. Together with Dino and John, I score in or near the middle range (53), which means that we can provide answers to both more existential questions focusing on the "why" (long term oriented) as well as a more short term focused reflection on questions related to the "how and the what", which are more likely to be asked by the team members having a short term oriented preference, such as Adrian, Erika and Yevgeni.

6. Indulgence

- The group shows a wide range in indulgence. Kalle (90), Adrian (84), Stefano (84), and Nick (84) exhibit high levels of indulgence, indicating a focus on enjoyment and pleasure.
- In contrast, members like Yevgeni (13) and John (38) are more restrained, prioritising discipline over pleasure-seeking.

The team's overall approach to balancing fun and seriousness pivots more towards enjoying life without too much restraint, which can be emotionally exhausting for more restrained team members such as Yevgeni and John. This means for myself (57) as manager that I need to keep an eye out for their emotional wellbeing.

Final thoughts

As we reflect on the journey through this book, one key theme has consistently emerged: The need to embrace the sense of "foreignerness" in today's increasingly globalised work environments.

Whether through our analysis of cultural dimensions, scenario-building, or strategic leadership insights, it is evident that embracing diversity is not just a corporate imperative but a human one.

Cultural diversity brings richness, innovation, and resilience to teams, but it also introduces challenges that can lead to isolation, misunderstandings, or a sense of otherness—the very "foreignerness" we seek to counter. Throughout the book, we've explored various tools and techniques to help individuals navigate these differences, from personal self-reflection on cultural values to visualising team landscapes through tools like the *"Landscape analysis"* and *"heat maps"* that reveal cultural tendencies.

For individuals, this means taking an active role in seeking out common ground with colleagues.

By identifying those who share similar cultural traits, whether it's a preference for long-term planning, a comfort with ambiguity, or a drive for achievement, individuals can foster a sense of belonging within diverse teams. As we've demonstrated through the examples of our interviewees, finding these cultural "anchors" within a team is key to reducing the feeling of foreignerness and enabling more harmonious collaboration.

For managers, the insights from previous chapters emphasise the importance of leveraging cultural differences as assets rather than obstacles.

Managers must approach diversity not as a challenge to overcome, but as an opportunity to create more dynamic, inclusive, and high-performing teams.

By acknowledging and strategically using the variety of cultural dimensions—such as hierarchical preferences, uncertainty avoidance, or indulgence—managers can tailor their leadership styles to better suit the needs of their teams.

In a perfect case (when building a whole new organization or team, for example) looking for managers with value preferences in the middle bandwidth enables an organization to optimise for a culturally diverse team, as the manager is more likely to be able to bridge value gaps between members.

This means employing situational leadership, understanding when to provide structure and when to allow autonomy, and balancing task orientation with relationship-building. By using cultural tools such as the *DDEE cycle*, managers can ensure that all voices are heard, fostering inclusion while still maintaining the necessary speed and decisiveness that a team requires to succeed.

Ultimately, countering "foreignerness" is about *bridging gaps*—not by erasing differences, but by making space for them, understanding them, and, where possible, aligning them.

As we've learned, individuals and managers alike must become cultural navigators, equipped with the insights to find common ground while appreciating the diversity that drives innovation and growth. Only then can we truly build teams where every individual feels both a sense of belonging and the freedom to be different.

www.ingramcontent.com/pod-product-compliance
Lightning Source LLC
Chambersburg PA
CBHW071500220526
45472CB00003B/865